The Interpretation of
Multiple Observations

The Interpretation of Multiple Observations

F. H. C. Marriott

Fellow of Wolfson College, Oxford

1974

ACADEMIC PRESS

London   New York   San Francisco

A Subsidiary of Harcourt Brace Jovanovich, Publishers

ACADEMIC PRESS INC. (LONDON) LTD.
24/28 Oval Road,
London NW1

United States Edition published by
ACADEMIC PRESS INC.
111 Fifth Avenue
New York, New York 10003

Library of Congress Catalog Card Number: 74-5652
ISBN: 0-12-473450 2

MADE AND PRINTED IN GREAT BRITAIN BY
THE GARDEN CITY PRESS LIMITED
LETCHWORTH, HERTFORDSHIRE
SG6 1JS

Preface

This book is intended for anyone who has to interpret collections of multivariate data. Its aim is to discuss critically the most important of the numerical methods available, and to relate them to the types of data for which they are suitable, and explain the questions they are trying to answer and the assumptions they involve.

Far too often, in theses, books and published papers there is evidence that the analysis was unsuitable, either because it was concerned with the wrong questions, because the procedure involved assumptions that the data did not justify, or because facts relevant to the interpretation were not incorporated with the data. Finally, even when the right method is used, the results must be interpreted, and mistakes occur at that stage. Statistical methods can be a real help in assimilating and organizing numerical results, but it is essential to understand what is going on.

The first part of the book, Chapters 2–6, deals with classical techniques, mainly established in the 1930s, but not widely used until recently because of the heavy computations involved. Chapters 7 and 8 discuss two more recent developments, the use of measures of similarity or dissimilarity, and the various methods of dividing items into groups, known as cluster analysis or classification analysis. Chapter 9 describes in some detail three examples of multivariate methods, chosen to illustrate the different approaches possible.

I have kept the mathematics to a minimum, quoting many results without proof, and in particular leaving out all the distribution theory. The statistical tests of the classical methods are well established, and can be used without knowing the derivations, provided the assumptions are satisfied. The theory can be found in the references given, particularly in Kendall and Stuart (1968) or Rao (1965). One aspect of the mathematics, however, is so important that it could not be left out; some understanding of matrices, and of methods of handling linear equations, is almost essential for the appreciation of the mechanics of the various techniques and of how computer programs handle the data. In Appendix A, I have outlined the elements of matrix theory that are most important in multivariate statistics.

On the other hand, I have assumed a reasonable familiarity with elementary (univariate) statistics. There are many text-books of statistical methods available; Pearce (1965) is one of the best. Many of the methods described here are generalizations of elementary techniques, and can be appreciated much more easily if the simpler cases are understood. In Appendix B I have described the basic univariate problem of linear inference, multiple regression, with some of its particular applications.

I have not attempted to discuss any specific case histories of applications of multivariate methods, apart from the three illustrative examples given in Chapter 9. Blackith and Reyment (1971) give an excellent selection of examples, from many different disciplines, published up to that time, and new instances appear in the literature every month. I have included no computer programs; most computer libraries have a wide selection of multivariate programs, and there are many more available. Hope (1968) and Blackith and Reyment (1971) offer a considerable selection.

In conclusion, I hope this book will help scientists to understand and interpret their data. If a numerical analysis gives answers that do not seem to make sense, something has gone wrong. There is no magic in these methods, and no reason to believe an answer because it comes from a computer. Interpretation needs skill, understanding and experience, and there are no short cuts.

Acknowledgements

My thanks are due to Professor C. B. Winsten and the *Journal of the Royal Statistical Society*, to Professor D. G. Kendall and *Nature*, and to Dr. R. Webster and *Soil Science* for permission to reproduce the figures on pages 8, 57, and 88 respectively.

I also gratefully acknowledge the help of the staff of Academic Press, who have dealt quickly and efficiently with an untidy manuscript.

June, 1974   F. H. C. MARRIOTT

Contents

Talking of shaving the other night at Dr. Taylor's, Dr. Johnson said, "Sir, of a thousand shavers, two do not shave so much alike as not to be distinguishable." I thought this was not possible, till he specified so many of the varieties in shaving;—holding the razor more or less perpendicular;—drawing long or short strokes;—beginning at the upper part of the face, or the under—at the right side or the left side. Indeed . . . we may be convinced how many degrees of difference there may be in the application of a razor.

Boswell's Life of Johnson

1
Introduction

A. SCOPE OF MULTIVARIATE ANALYSIS

Univariate statistics is concerned with the distribution of a single "variate", or random variable, specified by a frequency distribution giving the probabilities with which it takes each of its possible values. Multivariate statistics is concerned with the joint distribution of several variates.

Thus, for example, multiple regression is a problem in univariate statistics. Only one of the variables involved need to be a variate—namely the dependent variable. The others may be either controlled variables, with values set by the experimenter, or they may be variates, but in any case their distribution does not come into consideration. The only distribution involved is the distribution of the dependent variable about a mean value specified by the independent variables.

On the other hand, finding confidence limits for a correlation coefficient involves the assumption that the variables have a bivariate normal distribution (or possibly some other specified joint distribution). It is therefore a problem in multivariate statistics. Another problem that involves a joint distribution is that of finding a linear relationship between two variables when both are subject to random errors—the functional relationship problem.

Much of the mathematics involved in multivariate statistics is not new. The fundamental distributions related to the multivariate normal distribution were derived in the 1930s, and the methods developed then are the basis for most of the multivariate methods used today. Unfortunately, the calculations involved become extremely heavy when the number of variables is large, and the time required for them made it virtually impossible to carry them out on an electric calculating machine for more than about four or five variables. Until about twenty years ago, only a very limited number of multivariate analyses had been carried out, and the same examples were quoted in almost all the text-books.

The electronic computer has completely changed the situation, and

1

nowadays programs are available on almost all computers for almost all the principal multivariate methods. The results of multivariate analyses are published every week, and nobody need be deterred from carrying out an analysis by lack of computing facilities.

There remains the problem of deciding how to organize the data for computing, what type of analysis to carry out, and how to interpret the results when they are obtained. These are the questions that this book will be concerned with.

B. TYPES OF DATA

The first problem is that of putting the data into a form suitable for a digital computer. Several different types of variables may be involved, and they may require different treatment. In any case, they must be coded in a numerical form suitable for the particular program to be used.

1. Continuous variables

A continuous variable, strictly, is one that can take all values in a certain range (which may be infinite). The data, of course, are never continuous in this sense. Measurements are always made with limited accuracy, and there is always some degree of rounding off. The practical difference between continuous and discrete variables depends on the chance that different observations take the same value. For example, counts that follow a Poisson distribution with a large mean can, for practical purposes, be regarded as continuous, since only a small proportion of the observations will take any one value. On the other hand, a continuous variable grouped so coarsely that only, say, five or six values actually occur, must, at least for some types of analysis, be treated differently.

Another rather common type of variable is one that takes a wide range of values, but has a concentration at one value (usually zero). A typical example is counts of parasites on a host. It is usually better to regard such a variable as discrete, and score it as if it were a few groups—say zero, low, medium, and high.

Continuous variables do not present any particular problems. Generally they can be regarded as, to a reasonable approximation, jointly normally distributed, either in their original form or after a suitable transformation, and provided all the data are of this type, standard methods can be used.

2. Grouped data

Data may be coarsely grouped either because measurements are made with very limited accuracy, or because they are not made at all, and are replaced by rough assessments such as high, medium, low, or scored on some arbitrary scale. For many purposes, this grouping is not important. The assessment can be replaced by suitable scores, giving whatever weight is considered appropriate to the differences between the groups. In many of the classical multivariate methods the central limit theorem then justifies treating them as if they were jointly normally distributed. This point will be discussed in more detail in the next chapter.

There are, however, some applications in which care is needed. This is the case especially in cluster analysis. If the aim of an analysis is to find a useful or meaningful grouping of the data, a coarsely grouped variable may exert a disproportionate influence on the result.

3. Binary variables

One important special case of grouped data is that of observations that can take only two values, usually scored 0 and 1. These include such dichotomies as male and female, presence or absence of a feature, and other divisions into two groups. Often they can be treated in the same way as other grouped variables; just as in univariate applications the standard error of a proportion can be used for significance tests and confidence intervals as if the proportion were normally distributed, so in the multivariate case the central limit theorem often justifies treating binary data as approximately multivariate normal.

When, however, *all* the data are of this type, other models are available, and some special methods have been evolved for these cases.

4. Subdivisions

Often an observation may consist of a division into groups that are not logically ordered. For example, suppose flowers may be red, white, or blue. There is no logical reasons for scoring the colour by means of a single variable; to score these groups as 0, 1, 2 would imply that the white group was intermediate between the other two, and—unless, of course, there is some reason to believe this is so—it might be misleading.

One way of dealing with unordered groups of this sort is to replace them by binary variables. These three colours could be represented by two binary variables, one taking the value 1 for red flowers and 0 for white and blue, the other 1 for white and 0 for red and blue. These variables would, of course, be negatively correlated, since they cannot both be 1, but this does not matter.

Unordered groups can always be replaced by dummy binary variables in this way, but the device becomes rather cumbersome if there are many such groupings, or many groups involved. The method can also be misleading if it is used in conjunction with an analysis that does not take account of the correlations between variables (some types of cluster analysis, for example) since it may give undue weight to a subdivision into a large number of groups. An alternative approach is to base the analysis on a measure of distance or similarity, and this is probably preferable in most cases when there are many observations of this sort.

5. Missing variables

The problem of missing observations is common in univariate statistics, and as a rule can be dealt with quite easily by standard methods. A more difficult problem that is particularly important in numerical taxonomy is that of variables that cannot be observed when another variable takes a particular value.

Suppose, for example, that data are available on a group of insects, and some of the data relate to the venation of the wing. Some species may be wingless, and it is convenient to represent this condition by a binary variable taking the value 1 for winged species and 0 for wingless. Whenever it is 0, all the variables relating to the wing are missing.

There is no generally satisfactory way of dealing with this question. On the whole, methods based on measures of distance or similarity are more flexible than classical types of analysis in handling data of this sort, and this is one important reason for their popularity. Even using these methods, however, many difficulties remain, and the measure of similarity adopted must depend to some extent on an assessment of the relative importance of the variables. If it is thought that winglessness is an important character—one that has probably only arisen once in the course of evolution—it will be given considerable weight in the distance measure and the wingless species will be unlikely to be subdivided. On the other hand, it may be felt that winglessness is an aberration easily produced by the environment, and that the wingless species should be associated with whichever of the other groups they most resemble. In this respect, as in others, numerical methods in taxonomy cannot be completely mechanical.

6. Non-parametric methods and ranked data

In multivariate statistics, the distinction between parametric and non-parametric methods is often a little blurred. The classical techniques depend on the assumption of a multivariate normal distribution, but are reasonably robust for many types of data, and are often quite legitimately used for grouped or arbitrarily scored variables. Methods depending on distance measures, and clustering techniques that produce a dendrogram, are usually non-parametric. There are one or two specifically distribution-free methods, such as Kendall and Stuart's (1968) discrimination procedure. On the whole, however, the objective is to produce some description of the underlying features of the data, and the estimation of parameters is a secondary matter.

One rather common type of data consists entirely of ranked variables. It may arise either because the data are collected in this form, or because it is felt that the actual measurements have little meaning, and that nothing is lost by replacing them by ranks.

For many purposes, since samples are usually large, the crude ranks can be treated as if they were normally distributed. This has the disadvantage that ranks depend on sample size, and a discriminant function based on ranks will have a different set of values when applied to another sample of a different size. For this reason, it is often more convenient to transform the ranks, either using the Fisher-Yates rank transformation (Fisher and Yates, 1938), or simply dividing the ranks by the sample size.

7. Concomitant observations

The use of concomitant observations in univariate statistics is a familiar procedure. A typical example is in animal experimentation, when the initial weight of an animal is often used to adjust the final weights at the end of the experiment, and so to improve the accuracy. The analysis of covariance used in this way is a familiar and useful tool, and presents no special difficulties.

In multivariate statistics, concomitant observations can also be used. For example, in medical applications observations of age, sex, social status, and so on are often available as well as actual signs and symptoms of disease. Now, if the problem is to decide whether the disorder should be regarded as a single, homogeneous group, or whether it is made up of two or more separate syndromes (a problem in cluster analysis), it is clear that these subsidiary observations should not be regarded as on the same footing as the symptoms, but should be treated as concomitant observations.

If, however, it is known that there are two distinct diseases, and the problem is to discriminate between them on the basis of the observations, the question is less clear. It may be that one of the diseases is more common among males, and that sex is a definite factor in discrimination, or sex may affect the incidence of the different symptoms and so be more appropriately regarded as a concomitant observation.

These points will be discussed in more detail later. For the moment, the important point to realize is that multivariate data cannot be fed into a computer program regardless of their nature and relationship to the problem.

8. Graphical presentation

The principal aim of multivariate methods is the better understanding of the underlying structure of the measurements, and graphical presentation is perhaps the most important way of gaining such an understanding. Unfortunately, if p variables are observed, a scatter diagram to display them usually requires p dimensions. This is obviously impracticable when p is large, and it is important to consider how to present such data graphically with as little loss of information as possible.

(a) Multidimensional graphs. Graphical presentation is not restricted to two dimensions. There are various ways of representing data involving observations on at least three or four variables without any mathematical sophistication.

In the first place, it is easy to construct three-dimensional models. Winsten and Savigear (1966) have suggested a simple technique using pins of various heights, and have discussed the advantages of models of this sort.

Secondly, three-dimensional data may be represented on ordinary graph paper by using different symbols for different levels of the third variable. Figure 1.1 gives a simple example of this technique. The third variable has been grouped into high, medium, and low classes, and these are represented by large, medium, and small dots. Variations using shaded or coloured symbols may be used in the same way. Alternatively, the different levels of the third variable may be presented on different graphs, which are then to be imagined superimposed at different levels. Figure 1.2 shows the same data as Fig. 1.1 presented in this way. Figure 1.3 shows a pin-model, from Winsten and Savigear (1966).

Clearly, these methods may be combined to give graphs of four- or even five-dimensional data, but further extension is probably impracticable—the technique becomes too cumbersome, and the interpretation too difficult.

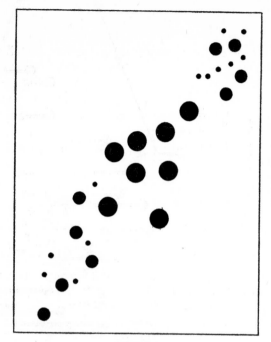

Fig. 1.1

A "three-dimensional" plot. The points constitute a scatter diagram for the values of two variables x and y; the value of the third variable, z, has been coded as low, medium, and high, and these are represented by small, medium and large dots.

The plot brings out the feature that the large z-values tend to form a compact group near the central values of x and y, while the smaller values form two groups, corresponding to low and high values of x and y.

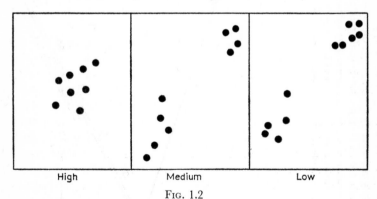

High   Medium   Low

Fig. 1.2

The same data as Fig. 1.1 plotted on three separate diagrams corresponding to high, medium and low values of z. This plot suggests still more clearly the two distinct groups for low and medium values of z, but it is less easy to visualize the x–y relationship when all the observations are plotted together.

Fig. 1.3

A pin-model, reproduced from the paper by Winsten and Savigear (1966). The three axes show the percentage of children under 15, the socio-economic index, and the room occupancy. The boroughs are indexed by the number at the foot of the pin, and the type is indicated by the pin head; the original figure is printed in two colours, and the heads are much more easily distinguishable. In addition, markings on the pin steams indicate the effect on occupancy of excluding furnished accommodation. This is a remarkable illustration of how much information can be conveyed in a single diagram without the detail becoming confused.

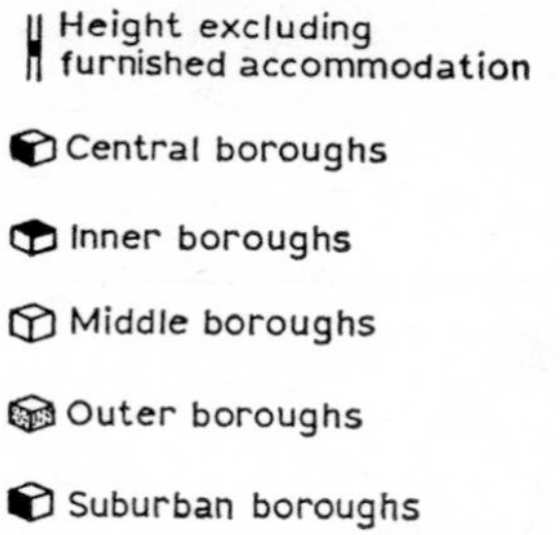

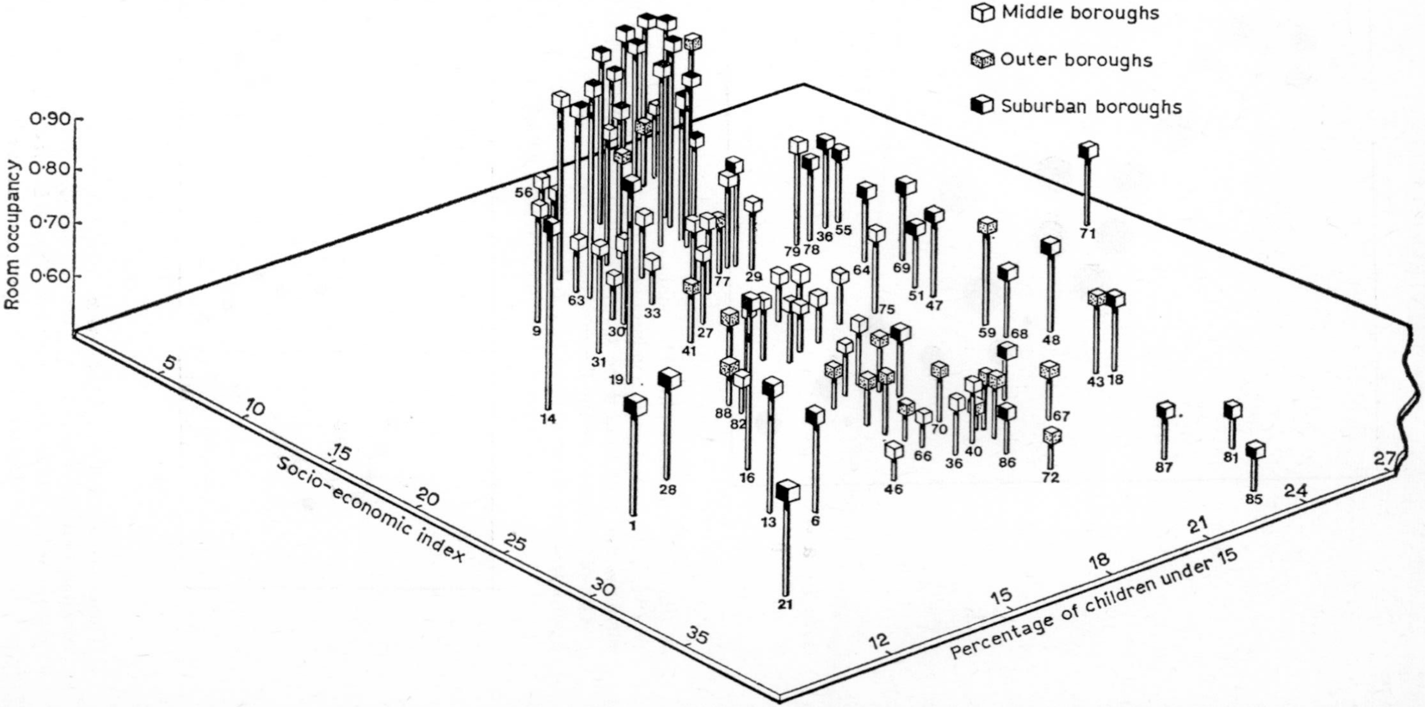

(b) Reduction of dimensionality. Various mathematical techniques have been devised with the main purpose of reducing the most important features of a set of data to a smaller number of variables. *Principal component analysis* is perhaps the most important. The original set of variables is replaced by a set of linear combinations arranged, in order, to account for as much of the variability as possible. It is then usual to plot the first few principal components in pairs, and try to interpret the results from these graphs. Clearly, it would be better to plot three or four simultaneously.

Another procedure for reducing dimensionality is *multidimensional scaling*. This is based on the distances between the points; the aim is to produce a representation in fewer dimensions that distorts the pattern of these distances as little as possible. The technique is closely related to principal component analysis.

(c) An entirely different approach has been suggested by Andrews (1972). The basis of his technique is to represent a set of multivariate data by a wave pattern, using Fourier analysis to transform the results into this form. The potentialities of the method have not yet been fully explored; at first sight, it seems to have great possibilities, but some experience and insight are needed to interpret the graphs.

C. PROBLEMS AND METHODS

1. Introduction

The purpose of any multivariate analysis is to gain some insight into the structure of the situation and the main features of the data. This may take various forms. It may be required to divide the data into groups, or to decide whether a known grouping is associated with the measurements. Alternatively, it may be possible to fit some definite mathematical model to the results. It may be that the measurements are of two types, and it is required to associate one with the other. All these situations need different types of analysis, and it is important to know exactly what questions are to be answered, and what sort of analysis can answer them.

2. Reification

When the mathematical analysis is finished, it is necessary to interpret it in terms of the original scientific problem. In particular, many of the mathematical techniques give rise to combinations of the original observations, and if these combinations can be interpreted in physical terms, it will aid comprehension of the results. For example, in soil science or plant ecology, one principal component might be associated with "drainage", another with "soil acidity", and so on.

This sort of interpretation is called reification. It must be emphasized that no mathematical method is, or could be, designed to give physically meaningful results. If a mathematical expression of this sort has an obvious physical meaning, it must be attributed to a lucky chance, or to the fact that the data have a strongly marked structure that shows up in the analysis. Even in the latter case, quite small sampling fluctuations can upset the interpretation; for example, the first two principal components may appear in reverse order, or may become confused together.

Reification, then, requires considerable skill and experience if it is to give a true picture of the physical meaning of the data. Essentially, it is a job for the experimental scientist rather than the statistician, who can do no more than give some guidance about what to look for, and what elaborations of the mathematical results are permissible.

3. Reduction of dimensionality

Techniques for reduction of dimensionality have already been mentioned in the last section. The chief methods are *principal component analysis* and various *scaling* or *ordination* procedures. The purpose of expressing the main content of the data in fewer dimensions is to make it easier to understand and to handle mathematically. In the first place, it is an essential preliminary to graphical presentation. Secondly, if there are redundancies in the original data, so that the variables are linearly related, either exactly or very nearly exactly, difficulties arise in the numerical analysis, and these can be eliminated by reducing the number of variables. Thirdly, the variables resulting from the reduction may lend themselves to reification, with a useful insight into the structure of the results.

4. Discrimination

The purpose of discriminant analysis is to investigate the relationship between a known grouping of the data and the variables recorded. The outcome of the analysis is an *allocation rule*, often, but not necessarily, associated with the values taken by a *discriminant function*. This rule can then be used for assigning to their appropriate groups the members of subsequent samples. With any allocation rule there is associated a certain probability of misclassification, and it is useful to be able to estimate this probability, at least roughly, and, of course, to choose the rule to make it as small as possible. Tests of significance show whether any real discrimination is possible; that is, whether the probability of misclassification is really less than would be achieved by random allocation.

5. Factor analysis

Factor analysis is designed to explain a set of multivariate data in terms of a fairly small number of underlying factors. It is a technique originally developed in the field of educational psychology; unlike most of the other methods discussed here, it involves fitting a definite mathematical model to the results, and if the conclusions are to have any meaning, the assumptions underlying the model must be strictly true. The model has proved its worth in the original field of application. Factor analysis has also sometimes been used in other fields—for example, in biology and geology—but here the model has much less obvious appeal, and great care is needed to be sure that the assumptions are reasonable.

6. Cluster analysis

Fairly recently a number of techniques have been developed for dividing data into groups. In this book they are discussed under the general heading *cluster analysis*, but the nomenclature is rather confused —the terms classification, dissection, and numerical taxonomy all being used to refer to the same process. The purpose of cluster analysis is to divide the data into groups, usually in the hope of detecting some sort of natural grouping, but possibly merely for the convenience of having smaller subdivisions.

A second product of some types of cluster analysis is a *dendrogram*, a pictorial representation of the data in the form of a family tree. This sort of graph has an obvious attraction for taxonomists, who are accustomed to identifying species by means of trees of a similar type, but its relation to the problem of optimum grouping, and its value in revealing relationships among the data, are not always clear.

7. Relationship between two sets of variables

Multiple regression is the univariate technique for finding the relationship between a single variate and a set of related variables. It is natural to consider what extension of this procedure is possible to relate several variates to another set of variables (which may or may not be random variables). An example might be the problem of relating the fauna of an area to the environment—soil type, vegetation, climate, and so on.

The classical extension of multiple regression to the multivariate case involves calculating *canonical correlations* between *canonical variates*, which are linear combinations of the original variables.

Canonical analysis has found surprisingly few applications in its general form. It would appear well adapted to many situations in economics and ecology, and in other disciplines, and several papers have been written advocating its wider use. In practice, however, much the most usual application has been to the case when the second set of variables represent the differences between groups. Just as an analysis of variance "between" and "within" groups can be regarded as a special case of multiple regression, so the multivariate extension of analysis of variance can be treated by the methods of canonical analysis, and they are often used in connexion with discriminant analysis to investigate the relationship between a set of variates and a known grouping.

2

The Multivariate Normal Distribution

A. GENERALIZATION OF THE NORMAL DISTRIBUTION

The importance of the normal distribution in classical univariate statistics suggests that a generalization to the multivariate case may be equally valuable. Such a generalization is provided by the *multivariate normal distribution*. The distribution is given by the equation:

$$f(x_1, x_2, \ldots x_p) = K \exp \left\{ -\tfrac{1}{2} \sum_{r,s=1}^{p} \alpha_{rs} (x_r - \mu_r) (x_s - \mu_s) \right\}$$

or
$$f(\mathbf{x}) = K \exp \left\{ -\tfrac{1}{2} (\mathbf{x} - \boldsymbol{\mu})' \, \boldsymbol{\alpha} \, (\mathbf{x} - \boldsymbol{\mu}) \right\}$$

in matrix notation. In this expression, $\boldsymbol{\mu}$ represents the vector of means of the p variates, and $\boldsymbol{\alpha}$ is the matrix inverse to the dispersion matrix. The dispersion matrix is the matrix with elements equal to the variances and covariances of the p variates; it is thus a $p \times p$ symmetric matrix with $\tfrac{1}{2}p \, (p + 1)$ distinct elements.

The distribution thus involves $\tfrac{1}{2}p \, (p + 3)$ parameters, made up of the p variate means, the p variances, and the $\tfrac{1}{2}p \, (p - 1)$ covariances (or, equivalently, the correlations) between the variates.

The variances and covariances must satisfy certain inequalities; these are implied by the fact that the correlation between any two combinations of variates cannot exceed unity. This is equivalent to saying that the dispersion matrix (and its inverse) must be positive definite (or positive semi-definite in the degenerate case when one of the variates can be expressed as a linear combination of the others).

The estimation of the parameters from a sample presents no difficulties. The means are estimated by the sample means $\bar{x}_r$; the variances by

$$s_r{}^2 = \frac{1}{N - 1} \, \Sigma(x_r - \bar{x}_r)^2$$

13

and the covariances by

$$c_{rs} = \frac{1}{N-1} \, \Sigma(x_r - \bar{x}_r)(x_s - \bar{x}_s)$$

The correlation between any two variates is estimated as the covariance divided by the square root of the product of the variances. The sample dispersion matrix, and the sample correlation matrix with unit terms in the principal diagonal, must also be positive definite.

The distribution is symmetrical, with a single mode at the point where all the variables have their mean value, and the density falls away steadily in all directions from this point. The distribution of each of the variates, and of any linear combination of them, is normal. Further, the joint distribution of any q linear combinations of the variates is multivariate normal.

The distribution is completely specified by the $\frac{1}{2}p \, (p + 3)$ parameters, and the sample estimates given are jointly sufficient for them; that is to say, they contain all the information about the population that can be obtained from the sample.

These properties are all simple extensions of corresponding properties of the normal distribution, or of the bivariate normal distribution.

B. THE MULTIVARIATE CENTRAL LIMIT THEOREM

The importance of the normal distribution in univariate statistics is due to the central limit theorem. This theorem states that if a variate x has any distribution with variance σ^2, the sample mean $\bar{x}$ of a sample of size N has a distribution that, as N increases, approaches a normal distribution with the same mean as x, and variance σ^2/N.

The central limit theorem is true for any distribution whatever with finite variance, but its practical importance is that it justifies the use of theory based on the normal distribution even when the distribution of x is not strictly normal—that is to say, for slightly skew distributions, for rectangular, binomial, and Poisson distributions, or any other distribution that has not too long a tail. It does not work in practice for observations with a few extremely large values, because the normal distribution is approached too slowly, and the approximation is valid only for unreasonably large values of N. These cases require a transformation.

The central limit theorem generalizes to the multivariate case in a fairly obvious way. If $x_1 \ldots x_p$ have variances $\sigma_1^2 \ldots \sigma_p^2$ and correlations p_{ij}, $i = 1 \ldots p$, $j = i + 1, \ldots p$, then the means $\bar{x}_1 \ldots \bar{x}_p$ of a sample of size N have a joint distribution that as N increases approaches a multivariate normal distribution with variances $\sigma_1^2 \ldots \sigma_p^2/N$, and with correlations ρ_{ij}, the same as those of the x's.

It is this theorem that gives the multivariate normal distribution its importance in multivariate statistics. It ensures that many of the statistical techniques and tests based on the multivariate normal distribution are robust, and will not give seriously misleading results even though the original data are not derived from a multivariate normal distribution. Some care is needed, however. Observations drawn from very long tailed distributions, with a few very large values, should be transformed using the same procedures as in the univariate case. Also, the protection afforded by the theorem does not extend to all procedures. In particular, cluster analysis based on the assumption of a mixture of multivariate normal distributions is sensitive to departures from normality, and some other calculations depend rather critically on the assumption.

C. THE WISHART DISTRIBUTION

The chi-squared distribution is the basis of all the univariate significance tests based on the normal distribution. The multivariate generalization of this distribution is the Wishart distribution, the joint distribution of the sample variances and covariances. This was discovered by Wishart (1928).

D. TESTS OF SIGNIFICANCE

Attitudes to tests of significance vary rather widely. At one extreme, biometricians sometimes make elaborate calculations without considering at all the accuracy that they might reasonably expect, or whether there is any real justification for the conclusions they reach. At the other, some workers give the impression that a statistically significant result is the complete answer to all problems, and that no further discussion is necessary.

Of course, the truth generally lies between these two extremes; the aim is to find a helpful model, simplification, or explanation of the results, that is largely independent of errors of measurement or sampling fluctuations. Exact significance levels are not of great importance, and it is true that the formulation of a null hypothesis sometimes seems an artificial and unnecessary procedure, but it is important to know that any parameters estimated have at least some meaning, and that conclusions based on one sample are unlikely to be contradicted by another.

One special difficulty arises in some forms of multivariate analysis.

Statistical tests are based on the concept of a random sample from a population, and this concept is not always realistic. Fisher introduced the idea of an imaginary infinite population, and used it with great freedom in cases where its applicability was far from obvious, but when the "sample" consists of all known species in a particular group, the postulation of an underlying "population" is stretching the imagination rather far. Other attempts to formulate the fundamental basis of statistics seem no more applicable to this sort of situation, and these considerations led Sibson (1972) to say that statisticians should concern themselves with some situations in which no element of probability was involved.

Nevertheless, the criteria used to assess statistical significance seem quite appropriate for deciding whether a group of species should be subdivided into genera or not. The taxonomist hopes that the differences between the groups he proposes will be greater than the variability within them, and hopes that this distinction will be "significant" in the non-statistical sense. He will hardly judge it so if the species might have been a random selection from a group containing all possible inter-mediates. It therefore seems reasonable to apply statistical significance tests to this sort of situation, not treating the 5% significance level as an infallible guide, but as a practically useful yardstick for deciding how far to proceed in the process of fragmentation.

E. HETEROGENEITY OF VARIANCES AND COVARIANCES: TRANSFORMATIONS

In univariate statistics, an important assumption in significance testing, for example in the t-test and the analysis of variance, is that the variance within groups is the same, and is independent of the mean. This assumption is much more critical than the assumption of normality. The latter may make significance levels inaccurate, but variance heterogeneity means that the test criteria used in the usual small-sample statistical tests are inappropriate.

On the other hand, the tests break down only when variance hetero-geneity is large and obvious. A test for homogeneity of variance (Bartlett's test) exists, but it is much less robust to non-normality than the tests it justifies; accordingly, it is not necessary to use it in a routine way as a necessary preliminary to an analysis of variance (Scheffé, 1959). It is quite legitimate to use the ordinary tests unless it is obvious that the means and variances are related, or it is known that the variate is distributed in a form in which this is the case.

In multivariate statistics, the corresponding assumption is that the dispersion matrices are the same—that is, that the variances and covariances are independent of the means and are the same within groups. Again, this assumption can be tested (Pearson and Hartley, 1972) but again this test is more sensitive than the procedures it is used to justify.

If it is clear that the assumption of homogeneity is not justified, it is necessary to transform the data. The theory of variance stabilizing transformations in the univariate case is well known (Bartlett, 1947a), and the same transformations can be used in the multivariate case. This will not, in general, remedy the situation if the correlations are dependent on the means, but this problem is less common, and I am not aware that any work has been done on it.

Much the most important transformation is the logarithmic. Instead of using the variable x in the calculations, it is replaced by $\log x$, and the calculations then proceed as before. This transformation is appropriate when the standard deviation of the observations is proportional to the mean, as very often happens with measurements of length or weight when the range is large. The transformation has the advantage that the conclusions have a fairly simple interpretation; the mean of $\log x$ is the log of the geometric mean of x, and the usual assumption of additive effects means that the effects on the original observations are multiplicative.

The logarithmic transformation is also useful when the data consist of counts, ranging from low to very high values. Such counts may arise, for example, from a negative binomial or a logarithmic distribution. There is one difficulty here: a zero count cannot be transformed in this way. The transformation is therefore varied by using $\log (1 + x)$ instead of $\log x$.

If the variance, instead of the standard deviation, is proportional to the mean, a square root transformation is appropriate. It is occasionally useful when counts follow a Poisson distribution.

Another type of transformation that can be used for almost any data consists in ranking the observations. This is the starting point of many non-parametric procedures in univariate statistics. In the multivariate case, it is often convenient either to treat the ranks as if they were jointly normally distributed, or to use the rank transformation of Fisher and Yates (1938), as discussed in the last chapter. This works well in most situations, but caution is needed when there are many tied ranks.

Little work has been done on transformations for multivariate data specifically, in which the transformed variates are functions of the original variates collectively rather than separately. Andrews *et al.* (1971) discuss the problem, and suggest techniques that can be used, at least when the number of variates is small.

3
Principal Component Analysis

A. PROCEDURE AND AIMS

The method of principal component analysis consists in transforming a set of variables $x_1 \ldots x_p$ to a new set $y_1 \ldots y_p$ with the following properties:

(i) Each y is a linear combination of the x's; say

$$y_i = a_{i_1} x_1 + a_{i_2} x_2 + \ldots + a_{ip} x_p.$$

(ii) The sum of squares of the coefficients a_{ij}, $j = 1 \ldots p$, is unity.

(iii) Of all possible combinations of this type, y_1 has the greatest variance.

(iv) Of all possible combinations of this type uncorrelated with y_1, y_2 has the greatest variance. Similarly, y_3 has the greatest variance of combinations uncorrelated with y_1 and y_2, and so on until the complete set of y's, from y_1 to y_p, has been defined.

In this way, a new set of p variables is defined, uncorrelated with each other, and arranged in order of decreasing variance. The main idea behind this procedure is that the first few principal components may well account for most of the variability in the original data, and for many purposes it may be reasonable to discard the remainder of them and so reduce the number of variables that it is necessary to consider.

The method is perfectly general; it involves no assumption about the original variables, no hypothesis that can be tested, no underlying model. It is simply a different, and possibly more convenient, way of expressing the same set of results.

B. MATHEMATICAL TREATMENT

If **V** is the matrix of variances and covariances—the sample dispersion matrix—the mathematical problem consists in finding the

18

vector $\mathbf{a}$ that maximizes the quadratic form $\mathbf{a'Va}$, subject to the constraint $\mathbf{a'Ia} = 1$. This implies (see Appendix A) finding a vector that satisfies $\mathbf{Va} = l\mathbf{a}$, where $| \mathbf{V} - l\mathbf{I} | = 0$. The last equation has p roots, and to each corresponds a different vector. Since $\mathbf{V}$ is positive definite, the roots are all positive, and when they are arranged in order, the largest root corresponds to the first principal component $\mathbf{a'x}$, the second largest root to the second principal component, and so on. Further, the variances of the principal components are equal to the corresponding values of l, the latent roots of the matrix $\mathbf{V}$.

The sum of the l's is equal to the sum of the elements of the principal diagonal of the matrix $\mathbf{V}$; that is to say, the sum of the variances of the principal components is the same as that of the original variables, and we may say that the first principal component accounts for a proportion $l_1/(l_1 + l_2 + \ldots l_p)$ of the total variance, and in the same way associate a proportion of the total variance with each of the principal components.

In this discussion, it has been tacitly assumed that the roots are all distinct and non-zero. Breakdown of these assumptions may complicate the numerical analysis, but most computer programs are designed to deal with such difficulties. The existence of a zero root implies, of course, that the original variables are linearly dependent; in this case, one or more of the principal components are simply zero. If there are two equal roots, the corresponding pair of principal components are not uniquely defined, but it is easy to find an uncorrelated pair that satisfy all the requirements.

The method of principal components has a simple geometrical interpretation. The equation $\mathbf{x'V^{-1}x} = K$ represents an ellipsoid in p dimensions. In fact, if the x's are variates with a multivariate normal distribution, these ellipsoids are the contours of equal probability density (centred on the common mean). The calculations involved in finding the principal components are then precisely those necessary to find the principal axes of the ellipsoid, in order of length. The case of equal roots corresponds to a circular cross-section, and a zero root means that the ellipsoid is degenerate, and could be represented in fewer than p dimensions.

C. STANDARDIZATION

It is important to realize that the method of principal components is not independent of scale. Multiplying one of the variates by a constant will change the dispersion matrix and produce a different set of principal components. In fact, there is not much point in carrying out an analysis of this sort unless the variates represent quantities of the same type with roughly similar variances, or unless they have been standardized in some way.

Cases when no standardization is needed are fairly common. Sometimes the variables are all of the same sort—all binary, all scored on a five-point scale, all percentages, all ratios of two lengths, or all measurements in the same units and of the same order of magnitude. In these cases, it is reasonable to regard the sum of the variances as a measure of overall variability, and attempt to account for it in terms of a smaller number of linear combinations of the variables.

One particularly important case is where the variables are all logarithms of lengths. The original measurements may be made on the whole organism, on different parts of it, or even on individual cells, and may differ by several orders of magnitude. The effect of the logarithmic transformation is to give measurements with the same *proportional* variability the same variance. In a sense, this is a variance-stabilizing transformation of the same sort as the log transformation discussed in the last chapter, but the aim here is not to stabilize the variance of a single variable throughout its range, but to make the variances of different variables comparable. At the same time, it is not a method of standardization; variables that are relatively more variable will have a higher variance and be given more weight in the following analysis.

Often the variables are observations of quite different types, recorded in different units or on different scales. In this case, a preliminary standardization is essential. The most usual method is to divide each variable by its standard deviation, thus reducing the variances to unity, and in effect working with the correlation matrix instead of the dispersion matrix. An alternative occasionally used is to standardize by the range. This seems less logical, since all the subsequent calculations are done with the variances; it has the effect of giving more weight to the more coarsely grouped variables, which, generally, does not seem desirable.

Standardization, as Kendall and Stuart (1968) point out, complicates the distribution theory and the sampling distributions. This point is of no practical importance, however; the theory when applied to actual data is at best approximate, and the error introduced by standardization is very unlikely to be important.

D. TESTS OF SIGNIFICANCE

It has been said that the calculation of principal components involves no assumptions about the relationships between the variables. Consequently, there are, as might have been expected, no important tests of significance associated with the technique.

There are, however, certain approximate tests (Bartlett, 1954) of some interest.

In the first place, if the variables are independently normally distributed with the same variance, then $-n \ln \{\mathbf{V}/(\mathrm{tr}(\mathbf{V})/p)^p\}$, where $\mathbf{V}$ is the sample dispersion matrix of the p variates, is approximately distributed as χ^2 with $\frac{1}{2}p \, (p+1) - 1$ d.f. If this test does not give a significant result, there is clearly no point in calculating principal components.

A similar test applied to the correlation matrix $\mathbf{r}$ tests whether the variates can be regarded as independent. If they are, $-n \ln |\mathbf{r}|$ is approximately distributed as χ^2 with $\frac{1}{2}p \, (p-1)$ d.f. (Bartlett, 1954).

The last test may be extended to test whether the first k latent roots account for all the interdependence between the variates. The test criterion is the ratio of the arithmetic to the geometric mean of the remaining latent roots $l_{k+1} \ldots . l_p$. If this ratio is R, then $n \, (p-k) \ln R$ is approximately distributed as χ^2 with $\frac{1}{2}(p-k-1) \, (p-k+2)$ d.f. For a refinement of this test, see Lawley (1956).

The third test is of some interest in connexion with the use of principal components in factor analysis. One point is worth emphasizing; there is no test that guides one in deciding whether some of the principal components can be ignored. This is a matter of judgment, and will be affected by knowledge of the accuracy of the observations, as well as the relative magnitude of the latent roots. Independence is not the primary criterion for rejection.

E. APPLICATIONS

1. Reification, size and shape, rotation

Sometimes, the first few principal components can be fairly convincingly identified with physical features of the original observations. As has been said, the mathematical treatment is not primarily directed to finding combinations of the observations that admit of easy interpretation, and quite often no simple reification is possible. If it is, however, the analysis may reveal directly interesting features of the data.

Suppose, for example, that in a principal components analysis of a series of soils, the first latent root is 60% of the sum of the variances, and suppose the variables that have the most weight in the corresponding principal component are all associated with drainage—clay content, mottling, stoniness (with a negative sign) and so on. One can then say that 60% of the total variability of the series of soils is associated with differences in drainage. This statement is informative and interesting. It is not mathematically precise, but reification is not a mathematical procedure; and it does tell us something about the soils examined. In the same way, if the second principal component is related to pH, and accounts for a further 20% of the total variance, one can make a similar statement about the importance of soil acidity, and so on.

It is important to realize the limitations of reification of this sort. The conclusions, including the order in which the components appear and the proportion of the variance associated with each, depend on the soils chosen and on the particular observations made and included in the analysis, as well as being affected by sampling variations. Statements like those in the previous paragraph usually have only a relative value; when similar sets of measurements have been made on several groups of soils, the importance of the principal components in the different groups can be compared.

Sometimes it happens that the individual components do not seem to suggest a simple reification, but a few of them, taken together, seem to be related to certain features of the data. For example, the largest weights in the first two components might seem to refer to observations connected with drainage and pH, although neither component is simply associated with either feature. It may be possible, however, to find two linear combinations of the components that *are* simply related to drainage and pH respectively. This procedure of combining vectors to find a meaningful expression is called *rotation*; its most important application is in factor analysis, in which, as will be seen, the factors are essentially indeterminate and reification is the main point of the analysis.

In connexion with reification, one often finds references to the concepts of "size" and "shape". Perhaps the clearest exposition of this idea is by Penrose (1954). Suppose the data consist of the logarithms of lengths measured on a series of organisms. It often happens that the coefficients in the first principal component are all positive, and all of the same order of magnitude. If so, it is natural to associate this component with the size of the organisms. Since the other principal components are uncorrelated with the first, they will tend to have about half positive and half negative coefficients. They are unrelated to size, and tend to reflect differences in the *shapes* of the organisms.

Penrose went on to propose a formal analysis in terms of size and shape, as an approximation to more precise, but computationally more difficult, techniques. This part of his paper has lost some of its import-

* *

ance with the development of computers and computer programs, but the underlying concept retains its value. As a rule, the taxonomist is not much interested in size, and so regards the first principal component as merely a means of eliminating this unwanted effect. The morphology is reflected in the second and later components.

The idea that the first principal component is a measure of size, in some sense, has gained considerable currency. Its value in the particular field of morphology is real, but it is only applicable in situations where the observations are all measurements of the same sort of thing. In other contexts, it has little meaning.

2. Graphical methods and cluster analysis

The use of principal components to reduce the number of dimensions so that graphical presentation of the data is possible has already been discussed. One of the most important applications is in connexion with cluster analysis. It is always difficult to define criteria by which to decide, using numerical methods, whether there is any justification for dividing a set of observations into groups. On the whole, the eye is more efficient at this sort of decision than the computer.

Plotting principal components can help with cluster analysis in several ways. In the first place, it may suggest a particular form of analysis: for example, if there are clearly defined and well separated groups, an elaborate analytical method is usually unnecessary. Then it may show why a particular technique has not given satisfactory results, and suggest alternatives. Finally, if no test of significance is possible, it may at least confirm that a suggested grouping looks reasonable, and is really indicated by the observations.

3. Redundancy

The standard techniques of multivariate analysis involve manipulating matrices of order equal to the number of variables. When the number is large, the calculations become heavy, even on modern computers. The difficulties are increased if correlations between the observations are high, so that the dispersion matrices are ill-conditioned or singular (see Appendix A).

One way of avoiding these problems is to do a preliminary principal components analysis, and discard the higher components. The analysis is then carried out on the retained components. There is then no problem with ill-conditioned matrices, since the new variables are uncorrelated. In many cases, the higher components contain more "noise" than "information", and little or nothing is lost by discarding them.

2—IOMO * *

There remains once more the problem of how many components to retain. It is not easy to give advice on this point. If the variables are first standardized, it may be reasonable to discard all components with a smaller variance than that of a single variable. On the whole, it is better to retain unimportant components than to discard information of value.

4. Factor analysis

Factor analysis and principal component analysis are both used to express the information contained in a set of observations in a smaller number of dimensions, and the relationship between the two is subtle. In many early papers, the method of principal components was used to estimate factors. Nowadays, other methods have been developed, and from one point of view, the first few principal components can be regarded as an approximation to the corresponding factors. On the other hand, if a slightly different model is adopted, principal components give in a perfectly valid sense the optimum estimates of the factors.

The relationship between the two techniques will be discussed in detail in the chapter on factor analysis.

F. PRINCIPAL COORDINATES

A variation of principal component analysis due to Gower (1966) brings out once again the duality between the p variates and the N individuals in a multivariate analysis. Principal component analysis is based on the $p \times p$ dispersion matrix, or the correlation matrix. Now suppose a_{ij} is some measure of similarity between the two *individuals i* and j (see Chapter 7). An $N \times N$ association matrix can then be defined, with elements a_{ij}. An analysis of exactly the same form as principal component analysis can then be based on this matrix, giving a set of vectors that are linear combinations of the individual's scores. These are called the *principal coordinates*. There will be N principal coordinates if $N \leqslant p$; otherwise $N - p$ of the latent roots will be zero.

The association matrix can be defined in many ways, but there are mathematical complications unless it is positive definite or semidefinite. Often, some form of correlation coefficient, based on the sums of squares and products of the scores of the two individuals, is used as a similarity measure.

The method of principal coordinates is primarily, like principal components, used for the reduction of dimensionality. There is in fact a close connexion between the two. If the first k principal components give an adequate representation of the data in k dimensions, and the remaining $p - k$ can reasonably be disregarded as uninformative "noise", then in the same way one can expect that the first k principal coordinates will have similar properties. When principal components are easy to extract and interpret, principal coordinates will usually contain just the same information, and nothing is to be gained by doing both calculations.

The real advantages of principal coordinates are those associated with the use of a similarity measure rather than variate values (see Chapter 7). In particular, when there are missing values, or missing variates, a correlation type of similarity measure is reasonably robust and reliable, while replacing the missing values by estimates or guesses is not very satisfactory.

Clearly, when N is large the calculation of principal coordinates is heavy, and if similar results can be obtained from the $p \times p$ dispersion matrix there is no point in carrying out the longer computations. On the other hand, if $N < p$ the calculation of principal coordinates is simpler.

It is in numerical taxonomy that the duality between individuals and variates is most important. Here, the number of characters observed is often large, and the "sample size", often in fact the population size, may be small. Missing values and variates are common, and similarity measures are often considered more reliable than variate values. In these circumstances, principal coordinates are preferable to principal components, and have exactly similar applications.

4
Canonical Variables

A. THE GENERALIZATION OF MULTIPLE REGRESSION

Multiple regression is concerned with the problem of the relationship of a single variate y with a set of variables $x_1 \ldots x_p$, which may or may not be random variables. The multivariate extension of this idea deals with the relationship of a set of variates with another set of variables. Suppose $x_1 \ldots x_p$ and $y_1 \ldots y_q$ are two sets of variables, one, at least, being random variables. When significance tests are involved, it will be assumed that this set is jointly normally distributed about a mean dependent on the other set. In fact, there is a symmetry about the relationship; it is unnecessary to specify which set consists of random variables, and without loss of generality we may take $p \leqslant q$.

Now, knowing the dispersion matrix of the complete set of $p + q$ variables, it is easy to calculate the correlation of any given linear combination of the x's with a given linear combination of the y's. Of all the possible pairs of linear combinations, one has the maximum correlation. This correlation is called the first *canonical correlation* and the corresponding pair of linear combinations of the x's and the y's are called the first *canonical variables*. (They have, of course, an arbitrary scale factor and an arbitrary mean, and it is usual to choose these constants so that each canonical variable has zero mean and unit variance.)

The second canonical correlation and variables are similarly defined by the pair of variables, uncorrelated with the first pair, that have maximum correlation, and so on until p pairs of canonical variables, and p canonical correlations have been defined. Thus we obtain p pairs of variables with the following properties:

(i) All the correlations among them are zero, except those between the corresponding pairs.

(ii) The correlations between the corresponding pairs form a decreasing sequence.

(iii) Each variable is standardized to have zero mean and unit variance.

The interpretation of the relationship between the two sets of variables is now based on these variables. It is possible to test whether there is evidence of any relationship, whether the relationship is accounted for entirely by the first, or the first few, pairs of variables, and whether some of the original variables can be left out of consideration without significantly affecting the conclusions. Reification of the canonical variables may be possible, and may clarify the nature of the relationship.

B. MATHEMATICAL FORMULATION

The calculation of canonical correlations and variables corresponds to a fairly difficult problem in matrix algebra, that of the simultaneous reduction of two quadratic forms to canonical form. This is discussed in Appendix A. Here, only the outline of the procedure will be given.

Suppose the dispersion matrix of the $p + q$ variables is partitioned, so that the $p \times p$ matrix $\mathbf{V}_{11}$ represents the variances and covariances of the x's, and $q \times q$ matrix $\mathbf{V}_{22}$ represents the variances of the y's, and the $p \times q$ matrix $\mathbf{V}_{12}$ (and its transpose $\mathbf{V}_{21}$) represents the covariances between the x's and the y's. Now if $\mathbf{a'x}$ and $\mathbf{b'y}$ are two linear functions of the x's and y's respectively, their variances and covariance are $\mathbf{a'V}_{11}\mathbf{a}$, $\mathbf{b'V}_{22}\mathbf{b}$, and $\mathbf{a'V}_{21}\mathbf{b}$. Then it is required to maximize $\mathbf{a'V}_{21}\mathbf{b}$ subject to $\mathbf{a'V}_{11}\mathbf{a} = \mathbf{b'V}_{22}\mathbf{b} = 1$. This leads to the equation

$$| \mathbf{V}_{21}\mathbf{V}_{11}^{-1}\mathbf{V}_{12}\mathbf{V}_{22}^{-1} - l\,\mathbf{I} | = 0.$$

Here, l is the undetermined multiplier in the maximization, and is, in fact the square of the correlation between the two new variables. The determinantal equation has p roots, and these give the values of the p canonical correlations, the positive square roots of the p values of l. To each canonical correlation there corresponds two sets of coefficients, and these can be found by solving the simultaneous equations:

$$\mathbf{V}_{21}\mathbf{V}_{22}^{-1}\mathbf{a'V}_{21} - l^2\mathbf{a'V}_{11} = 0$$
$$\mathbf{V}_{21}\mathbf{b}\mathbf{V}_{11}^{-1}\mathbf{V}_{21} - l^2\mathbf{V}_{22}\mathbf{b} = 0$$

The calculations involved are heavy if p and q are large, but they are usually well within the capacity of a large computer. There are the usual minor complications if one of the dispersion matrices is singular, or if two of the latent roots are equal, but they do not present any real difficulties.

C. TESTS OF SIGNIFICANCE

Tests of significance in canonical analysis are of two types. An overall test of significance, analogous to the F test in analysis of variance or multiple regression, may be based on all the canonical correlations, or one may test the largest correlation only. Both these tests may be extended to test for independence after one or more pairs of canonical variables have been eliminated.

The two types of test are, of course, concerned with the same null hypothesis. If the largest canonical correlation (in the population) is zero, the two sets of variables are completely uncorrelated, and all the population canonical correlations are zero. Which test is more powerful depends on the alternative hypothesis. If the relationship between the two sets is chiefly accounted for by a correlation between two linear functions of the variables—that is, by a single canonical correlation— a test based on the first canonical correlation l_1 will be more sensitive. A test based on all the correlations may fail to give significance because the effect of the first is swamped by the inclusion of the others. An example where this type of test is likely to be more powerful occurs when one set of variables represent a grouping in time. A regular change in a single linear function of the other set, representing perhaps changing size or shape, will show up as one large canonical correlation, while the others may all be small. The situation is analogous to a familiar one in univariate statistics; a non-significant F value should not deter one from examining particular contrasts of special interest.

If, on the other hand, the relationship between the two sets consists of several correlations between individual pairs of variables, or small groups of variables, the canonical analysis is not a very fruitful approach; none of the individual correlations may be large, yet the overall test of significance may show that the two sets are not independent.

The usual procedure in practice is to use the overall test first, and if it is not significant, check the result by a test on the first canonical correlation. If the overall test is significant, eliminate the first canonical correlation and test the remainder, testing the second if the remainder is not significant. This process continues until neither test gives a significant result, and it is clear that all the significant correlations have been identified.

The overall test of significance is based on *Wilks' criterion*. Perhaps the easiest way of expressing this quantity is to consider the regression of each of the x's separately on the y's. These regressions will give a set of residuals, and the variances and covariances of the residuals can be calculated. The original dispersion matrix of the x's was $\mathbf{V}_{11}$; if

the dispersion matrix of the residuals is $V_{11} = V_{11}* - V_{12}V_{22}^{-1}V_{21}$
Wilks' criterion is defined as $L = |V_{11}*| / |V_{11}|$. If there is little
correlation between the two sets of variables, L is near unity; if they
are closely correlated, L becomes small. It is easy to see that the same
quantity is defined by carrying out the same procedure on the y's if
$p = q$; otherwise the $q \times q$ determinants are both zero. In terms of the
latent roots l, the squared canonical correlations,

$$L = (1 - l_1)(1 - l_2) \ldots (1 - l_p).$$

An approximate test based on Wilks' criterion was suggested by
Bartlett (1938). The quantity $\{-n + \frac{1}{2}(p + q + 1)\}\ln L$ is approximately distributed as χ^2 with pq d.f. (where there are $n + 1$ observations
in all). This approximation is adequate for most practical purposes,
and the simplicity and flexibility of the χ^2 distribution leads to tests
of subsidiary hypotheses that are even more valuable than the general
test.

An exact test of Wilks' criterion is, of course, available when $p = 1$,
since the problem then reduces to that of multiple regression. In fact,

$$\frac{n - q}{q} \frac{1 - L}{L}$$

has an F distribution with q and $n - q$ d.f. An exact test for $p = 2$
was given by Wilks (1935). The quantity

$$\frac{n - q - 1}{q} \frac{1 - \sqrt{L}}{\sqrt{L}}$$

has an F distribution with $2q$ and $2(n - q - 1)$ d.f. For other values
of p, exact significance levels have been calculated by Schatzoff (1966)
(see Pearson and Hartley, 1972). These are given in the very convenient form of a correction factor C to be applied to Bartlett's test.
A glance at the tables shows that for reasonably large samples, C is
always very close to unity, so that for many purposes the refinement is
unnecessary.

Important extensions of Bartlett's test depend on partitioning the
χ^2 value to give tests of further hypotheses.

(i) To test whether the relationship between the x's and the y's can
be explained entirely by the first k canonical correlations, write

$$L = L_k L_{p-k},$$

where $L_k = (1 - l_1) \ldots (1 - l_k)$, $L_{p-k} = (1 - l_{k+1}) \ldots (1 - l_p)$.
Now the hypothesis can be tested by $\{-n + \frac{1}{2}(p + q)\}\ln L_{p-k}$,
which is approximately distributed as χ^2 with $(p - k)(q - k)$ d.f.

Notice that L_k does *not* give a significance test for the first k canonical correlations; the partition is based on the assumption that the first k sample canonical correlations do correspond to non-zero population values. Putting $k = 1$ does not give a test of the largest canonical correlation, but putting $k = p - 1$ does give a test of the smallest if the others are significant.

(ii) To test whether certain variables contribute significantly to the relationship, the value of χ^2 including and omitting these values are compared. Suppose k_1 x's and k_2 y's are omitted, and L^* is calculated for the remaining $(p - k_1)$ $(q - k_2)$ variables. Now

$$\{-n + \tfrac{1}{2}(p + q + 1)\}\ln L^*$$

is approximately distributed as χ^2 with $(p - k_1)$ $(q - k_2)$ d.f. (It is better not to change the multiplying factor, since the additive property of χ^2 is to be used.) Then $\{-n + \tfrac{1}{2}(p + q + 1)\}\ln L/L^*$ is approximately distributed as χ^2 with $pk_2 + qk_1 - k_1k_2$ d.f. This test, derived from the difference between the two χ^2 values for L and L^*, with d.f. equal to the difference between the d.f. for the two cases, tests whether the $k_1 + k_2$ variables can be left out of consideration. In particular, putting $k_1 = 1$, $k_2 = 0$ gives a significance test of one of the coefficients in the canonical variables, and by equating significance levels rough estimates of the standard errors of coefficients can be found.

Tests of this sort can be developed from Bartlett's original χ^2 test, and greatly extend the flexibility of the analysis. For a fuller discussion, see Bartlett (1947b).

For testing the largest latent root, Marriott (1952) showed that the criterion suggested by the partitioning of Bartlett's χ^2 test, namely $\{-n + \tfrac{1}{2}(p + q + 1)\}$ $\ln$ $(1 - l_1)$ followed approximately a χ^2 distribution with $p + q - 1 + \tfrac{1}{2}\{(p - 1)(q - 1)\}^{2/3}$ d.f. This is quite a convenient test to use, although the d.f. are in general non-integral, and significance levels require interpolation; for practical purposes, the accuracy is quite adequate when n is reasonably large. Exact significance levels, mainly due to Pillai, are given by Pearson and Hartley (1972).

Marriott's test can be used to test the kth canonical correlation, when the first k have been shown to be significant, simply by replacing p and q by $p - k$ and $q - k$. This gives the same test for the smallest root $(k = p - 1)$ as Bartlett's test above, apart from a small difference in the multiplying factor.

Finally, a test statistic proposed by Hotelling (1931) is occasionally used. Hotelling's T was originally proposed as a generalization of Student's t, and related to the case $p = 1$. Since an exact variance-ratio test is available for this case, the statistic is more or less obsolete in practical work, but the theory has been developed, and is of some importance in mathematical statistics, especially in connexion with comparisons of the powers of different tests.

D. APPLICATIONS

Applications of canonical analysis, in the typical form in which both sets of variables are continuous, are rare, as has already been pointed out. In cases when it might be expected to be useful it is often simpler, and equally informative, to carry out a multiple regression of each of the variables in one group on those in the other. Reification is easier in this case; otherwise it is necessary to explain simultaneously both canonical variables of each pair.

Canonical analysis is valuable because it gives the significance tests and sampling theory of classical multivariate statistics in a clear and symmetrical form. The most important applications in practice are when one set of variables is replaced by a division into groups. This problem will be discussed under the heading of discriminant analysis. Here the techniques and tests of this chapter are really valuable; canonical analysis is a generalization of multiple regression, and discriminant theory of analysis of variance within and between groups, and discriminant analysis can be regarded as a special case of canonical analysis in the same sense that analysis of variance within and between groups can be regarded as a special case of multiple regression.

5
Discriminant Analysis

A. AIMS AND ILLUSTRATIONS

The purpose of discriminant analysis is to examine how far it is possible to distinguish between members of various groups on the basis of observations made upon them. The data consist of the values of a set of random variables $x_1 \ldots x_p$ on $n + 1$ individuals which are divided into g (known) groups. The analysis provides:

(i) Tests of significance for differences in the values of the x's between the groups.

(ii) Allocation rules, for identifying further individuals as belonging to one of the groups on the basis of the values of the x's. These rules are often—but not necessarily—expressed in terms of *discriminant functions*.

(iii) Estimates of the probability of correct allocation, using the rules that have been derived.

Discriminant analysis is thus the extension to multivariate observations of the ordinary analysis of variance within and between groups. In the same sense that an analysis of variance of this sort can be regarded as a special case of multiple regression discriminant analysis can be regarded as a special case of canonical analysis. It presents, however, problems of its own in determining allocation rules and assessing their efficiency.

Two examples will illustrate the aims of the technique:

(i) Two diseases, A and B, are difficult to distinguish on the basis of the signs and symptoms. A definite diagnosis is possible only by a biopsy, but this involves a surgical operation. Data are available on a number of cases in which biopsy, or *post mortem* examination, has made the diagnosis certain. Discriminant analysis will determine how far diagnosis is possible without biopsy, and if some discrimination between the diseases can be made from the symptoms, will suggest how to decide whether biopsy should be performed.

(ii) Wood of a particular species is obtained from a number of different locations. An analysis of the characteristics of samples of known provenance may cast light on the effect of local conditions on the timber produced, and may make it possible to assign unknown samples to the appropriate locality.

B. MULTIVARIATE ANALYSIS OF VARIANCE

An analysis of variance between and within groups can be carried out in the usual way on each of the variates. In exactly the same way, the sums of products, $\Sigma(x_i - \bar{x}_i)(x_j - \bar{x}_j)$, can be split up into components within and between groups. This leads to an analysis of the following form:

	d.f.	S.O.P. matrix	Estimated dispersion matrix
Between groups	$g - 1$	**B**	
Within groups	$n - g + 1$	**W**	$\mathbf{V} = \mathbf{W}/(n - g + 1)$
Total	n	**S**	

in which the *matrix* **S** is expressed as the sum of matrices **B** and **W** of sums of squares and products between and within groups respectively. This is known as a multivariate analysis of variance, or sometimes as an analysis of dispersion. It takes exactly the same form as an ordinary analysis of variance and covariance, but the purpose is different. Here the aim is not to carry out an analysis on one variate with the effect of the others removed; all the x's are on the same footing.

If a new random variable is defined as a linear function of the x's, say

$$y = a_1 x_1 + \ldots + a_p x_p = \mathbf{a'x}$$

it is easy to carry out an analysis of variance on y. The components are **a'Ba**, **a'Wa**, which sum to **a'Sa**.

The matrix **V**, formed by dividing the elements of **W** by the degrees of freedom $n - g + 1$, is the estimated dispersion matrix within groups. The elements are unbiased estimates of the variances and covariances of the x's within groups.

C. DISCRIMINATION BETWEEN TWO GROUPS

If an observation **x** is derived from a multivariate normal distribution with dispersion matrix **A** and mean μ, the likelihood of **x**, or the probability density at **x**, is proportional to

$$\exp -\tfrac{1}{2}(\mathbf{x} - \mu)'\mathbf{A}^{-1}(\mathbf{x} - \mu)$$

Given two such distributions, with estimated means $\bar{\mathbf{x}}_A$ and $\bar{\mathbf{x}}_B$ and estimated dispersion matrix **V**, it is natural to assign **x** to whichever has the higher likelihood. Now the difference between the log likelihoods is estimated as:

$$Y = -\tfrac{1}{2}(\mathbf{x} - \bar{\mathbf{x}}_\mathrm{A})'\mathbf{W}^{-1}(\mathbf{x} - \bar{\mathbf{x}}_\mathrm{A}) + \tfrac{1}{2}(\mathbf{x} - \bar{\mathbf{x}}_\mathrm{B})'\mathbf{W}^{-1}(\mathbf{x} - \bar{\mathbf{x}}_\mathrm{B})$$

This reduces to

$$Y = (\mathbf{x} - \bar{\mathbf{x}})'\mathbf{W}^{-1}\mathbf{d}$$

where $\bar{\mathbf{x}} = \tfrac{1}{2}(\bar{\mathbf{x}}_\mathrm{A} + \bar{\mathbf{x}}_\mathrm{B})$, $\mathbf{d} = \bar{\mathbf{x}}_\mathrm{A} - \bar{\mathbf{x}}_\mathrm{B}$. This is a linear function of $\mathbf{x}$, positive when the likelihood of $\mathbf{x}$ is greater for group A, and negative when it is greater for B. It is called a linear *discriminant function* between the groups, and gives immediately the allocation rule: if $Y > 0$, assign $\mathbf{x}$ to A, if $Y < 0$, assign $\mathbf{x}$ to B.

This derivation shows that the appropriate function is a linear function of the x's. An alternative approach is to ask what linear function of the x's gives the greatest discrimination between the groups—that is, the function

$$\mathbf{a}'\mathbf{x} = a_1 x_1 + \ldots + a_p x_p$$

that maximizes $\mathbf{a}'\mathbf{B}\mathbf{a}$ for fixed $\mathbf{a}'\mathbf{W}\mathbf{a}$. For two groups,

$$\mathbf{B} = (n_\mathrm{A} + n_\mathrm{B})\,\mathbf{d}\mathbf{d}'$$

and maximizing $\mathbf{a}'\mathbf{d}\mathbf{d}'\mathbf{a} - l\mathbf{a}'\mathbf{W}\mathbf{a}$ gives $|\mathbf{d}\mathbf{d}'\mathbf{a} - l\mathbf{W}\mathbf{a}| = 0$ (see Appendix A). This is satisfied by $\mathbf{a} = \mathbf{W}^{-1}\mathbf{d}$, $l = \mathbf{d}'\mathbf{W}^{-1}\mathbf{d}$ which leads to the same discriminant function and allocation rule as before.

A third derivation is obtained by considering a variable y with the value $+1$ for group A and -1 for B. A regression of y on $x_1 \ldots x_p$ then gives the linear function of the x's that discriminates best between the groups. This method gives the same function again, multiplied by a constant factor. In fact, the regression coefficients

$$\mathbf{b} = \mathbf{a}/(1 + k\mathbf{d}'\mathbf{W}^{-1}\mathbf{d}),$$

where $k = n_\mathrm{A} n_\mathrm{B}/(n_\mathrm{A} + n_\mathrm{B})$.

To test the significance of a discriminant function, $L = |\mathbf{W}|/|\mathbf{S}|$ is Wilks' criterion (see Chapter 4). Now for $g = 2$,

$$F(p, n - p) = \frac{n - p}{p}\,\frac{1 - L}{L}$$

gives a significance test to determine whether there is any significant difference in the x's between the groups—that is, whether any effective discrimination is possible. It is easily seen that a formal F test for the regression procedure above gives the same test, and yet another form is given by the test of D^2 in the next section.

Finally, the discrimination function may be simplified by eliminating those variates whose coefficients are not significant. The easiest way of doing this is to use the regression approach.

D. THE GENERALIZED DISTANCE

The concept of the *generalized distance* between two populations was introduced by Mahalanobis, and its properties have been investigated chiefly by the Indian statisticians. Suppose **d** is the vector of differences between the x-means in groups A and B ($d_i = \bar{x}_{iA} - \bar{x}_{iB}$, $i = 1$

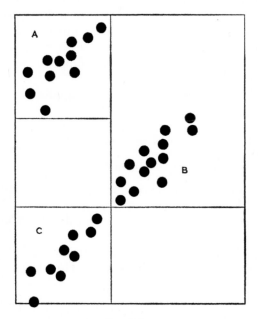

FIG. 5.1

The three groups A, B and C have similar dispersion matrices. The Euclidean distance between the means of A and B, and B and C, is about the same. The generalized distance, on the other hand, takes account of the scatter of the variables and of the correlations among them. The generalized distance between A and B is much greater than that between B and C.

... p). The statistic $D^2 = \mathbf{d'V^{-1}d}$ is the estimate of a corresponding parameter, dependent on the means of the two groups and the dispersion matrix within groups. This parameter is known as the squared generalized distance between the groups.

The generalized distance and its estimate have the following properties:

(i) They are scale-independent. The value of D^2 is unaltered if the x's are multiplied by arbitrary constants, or replaced by a set of p linear combinations which are not linearly dependent (e.g. the set of principal components).

(ii) They take account of correlations between the variates. For example, in Fig. 5.1, the distance between the means of A and B is about the same as that between B and C, but the *generalized* distance is much greater between A and B. This is in agreement with the fact that the contours of equal probability density are further apart; if the variances were greater, B and C would overlap much more than A and B.

(iii) The value of D is the difference between the mean values of the discriminant function, regarded as a linear function of the x's, for the two groups, divided by its S.D. (This, of course, does not give rise to a test of significance, since the discriminant function is chosen precisely to maximize the ratio.)

The distribution of D^2 is known, and a significance test for differences between the two groups is given by

$$F(p, n - g - p + 1) = D^2(1/n_A + 1/n_B)^{-1} \frac{(n - p - 1)}{p(n - g)}$$

where n is the total number of observations.

If $g = 2$, this is the same as the significance test for regression given in the last section, but it is a little more general, since it provides a test for the difference between any two groups when the S.O.P. matrix **W** is based on variation within g groups.

This test is a generalization to the p-variate case of the ordinary t-test. It is sometimes expressed in terms of Hotelling's T. If

$$T^2 = \frac{D^2}{1/n_A + 1/n_B}$$

a significance test is given by

$$F(p, n - g - p + 1) = T^2 \frac{n - p - 1}{p(n - g)}$$

When $p = 1$ and $g = 2$, this reduces to the ordinary t-test for the difference between the means of two groups.

The distribution of D^2 when the generalized distance in the population is not zero is based in the same way on the non-central F distribution (see Rao, 1965). The distribution has been used to compare distances based on different numbers of variates (Rao, 1950) or between corresponding groups in different populations.

E. PRIOR INFORMATION AND UNEQUAL RISKS

Sometimes information is available about the relative sizes of groups A and B, and the allocation rule can be modified to allow for it. Suppose the prior probabilities of A and B are p_A and p_B respectively, and the sample mean vectors are $\bar{\mathbf{x}}_A$ and $\bar{\mathbf{x}}_B$. The log probability density at $\mathbf{x}$ is estimated as $\ln p_A - \frac{1}{2}(\mathbf{x} - \bar{\mathbf{x}}_A)'\mathbf{V}^{-1}(\mathbf{x} - \bar{\mathbf{x}}_A) + C$ if $\mathbf{x}$ belongs to group A, plus a similar expression if it belongs to B. This suggests the discriminant function

$$\ln p_A/p_B - \tfrac{1}{2}(\mathbf{x} - \bar{\mathbf{x}}_A)'\mathbf{W}^{-1}(\mathbf{x} - \bar{\mathbf{x}}_A) + \tfrac{1}{2}(\mathbf{x} - \bar{\mathbf{x}}_B)'\mathbf{W}^{-1}(\mathbf{x} - \bar{\mathbf{x}}_B).$$

If $p_A = p_B$, the rule is exactly the same as that in Section C, but the interpretation is different. When the prior probabilities are known to be equal, the rule implies that it is *more probable* that $\mathbf{x}$ belongs to the group indicated. When they are not known, the value of $\mathbf{x}$ gives *more support* (a higher likelihood) to the allocation.

When $p_A \neq p_B$, the discriminant function is modified by adding a constant, $\ln p_A/p_B$. The plane dividing the points assigned to A and B is shifted, but not rotated.

Sometimes the consequences of wrong allocation are more serious in one direction than the other—the case of medical diagnosis provides obvious examples. Suppose the cost of wrongly allocating to B an individual of A is c_A, and the cost of the opposite error is c_B. A simple application of decision theory shows that the discriminant function should be modified by adding $\ln c_A/c_B$.

F. UNEQUAL DISPERSION MATRICES

The methods discussed so far in this chapter are based on the assumption that the x's are jointly normally distributed with a constant dispersion matrix. The assumption of normality is seldom justified, but the central limit theorem ensures robustness for almost any distribution in which the variance is independent of the mean (or of group membership). Heterogeneity of dispersion matrices is a much more serious matter.

As has been mentioned in the last chapter, there is no difficulty in testing for homogeneity, but the test is very sensitive to the assumption of normality, and so less robust than the tests it is supposed to justify or reject. Scatter diagrams of principal components will reveal any gross heterogeneity. If it exists, it can often be eliminated by a suitable transformation of some of the x's (Chapter 1). If not, a more radical change of method is necessary.

G. A DISTRIBUTION-FREE METHOD

Non-parametric methods have not been much used in discriminant analysis. The following technique is suggested by Kendall and Stuart (1968).

The range of each variate can be divided into three non-overlapping parts:

(a) one end containing members of group A only;
(c) a middle, containing members of A and B;
(b) the opposite end, containing members of group B only.

(If the extreme items belong to the same group, only (c) exists.)

Select as x_1 the variate with the largest number of items in (a_1) and (b_1).

Assign all observations in (a_1) to A, all in (b_1) to B. Record the innermost values of (a_1) and (b_1), and the first instruction in the allocation rule is to allot to A or B all items having values of x_1 outside these limits.

Select as x_2 the variate with the largest number of items *of* (c_1) in (a_2) and (b_2).

The second instruction in the allocation rule then allots items unallocated by x_1 in accordance with the value of x_2.

This process can be continued until either all items are disposed of or until all the variables have an item of the same group at both ends of their range. Richards (1972) has pointed out that there is no reason why a variate should not be used more than once in different steps of the rule.

This method is completely distribution-free; it depends only on the ranking of the separate variates. It is, however, clearly very inefficient when there are many variates and none of them individually discriminates efficiently. It could be modified, for example by considering discrimination by combinations of variates, but that would destroy some of its generality.

The real difficulty, however, is to know when to stop. It is necessary to decide whether the discrimination afforded by a particular variate is real, or merely a chance effect. Often some variates will show differences that are obviously significant, but to decide whether the ranking associated with the best of a number of measures—not, of course, independent—could be a chance effect or not is difficult. A possible solution is to adopt some arbitrary rule, and check the results by the method of Section I below.

H. QUADRATIC DISCRIMINANT FUNCTIONS

Another approach to the problem of unequal dispersion matrices is to adopt a generalization of the ordinary large-sample procedure for testing the difference between two means. The discriminant function

$$\ln \frac{p_A c_A}{p_B c_B} - \tfrac{1}{2}(N_A - 1)\,(x - \bar{x}_A)'W_A^{-1}\,(x - \bar{x}_A)$$
$$+ \tfrac{1}{2}(N_B - 1)\,(x - \bar{x}_B)'W_B^{-1}\,(x - \bar{x}_B)$$

in an obvious notation, is the natural generalization to adopt. This is, of course, a *quadratic* discriminant function, and its use has certain interesting features.

In the first place, it must be emphasized that large samples are necessary in all groups. There is a real risk of quite spurious discrimination because in the sample one variate has an exceptionally low variance, or a group of variates have high correlation, in two groups. The risk increases with the number of variates and with the number of groups, and while a large sample univariate test is valid with 20 or so in each group, in the multivariate situation large sample methods imply much larger numbers.

In some cases, the surface dividing the items allotted to A and B may be ellipsoidal, and the points allotted to one group may be completely enclosed by those allotted to the other. This is the case, in particular, when the groups differ in variability but not in mean. If the prior probabilities, or the costs, differ, the ellipsoid may degenerate so that all points are allotted to one group.

When the correlations within the groups differ, the dividing surface may be more complex—in three dimensions, a hyperboloid of either one or two sheets. When the means and dispersion matrices are independently estimated for more than two groups, quite bizarre situations can arise, with several isolated sections of space allotted to a single group.

All this seems remote from any practical discrimination problem. In fact, the underlying assumption of multivariate *normal* distributions with differing means and dispersion matrices is hardly realistic. In practice, it is almost always possible to transform the data in such a way that the dispersion matrices are not grossly different, and then deal with the problem using linear discriminant functions.

I. ESTIMATION OF THE PROPORTION MISCLASSIFIED

The success of a discriminant function analysis can be judged by estimating the proportion of the population which would be correctly classified. There are two ways of doing this. The estimate may be based either on the proportion of the assumed multivariate normal distribution on either side of the plane defined by the discriminant function, or on the proportion of the sample actually on either side of the plane.

By the first method, the probability of misclassification corresponds to a normal deviate of $\frac{1}{2}D$. Thus if $D^2 = 16$, $\frac{1}{2}D = 2$, and the proportion of each group misclassified by the best linear discriminant function is 0·023.

This method is the only one possible when the sample is not large. It is open to the objection that it relies on the assumption of normality, with no protection from the central limit theorem. This is not usually a serious fault when the proportion misclassified is fairly large, but when D is large, the estimate of the tail of the distribution may be seriously in error, in either direction.

The alternative method is simply to count the actual members of the sample that would have been misclassified by using the allocation rule derived. This obviously gives a biased estimate; the rule is based on the particular sample, and is likely on the whole to give better results for it than for other samples, or for the population as a whole.

The bias is unlikely to be serious for large samples. It can be removed by a procedure due to Hills (1966). Each item is removed from the sample in turn, an allocation rule is calculated for the remaining n, and the removed item classed as correct or incorrect on the basis of this rule.

This procedure certainly removes the bias, but the extra computation involved is heavy, and seldom worth while. It seems, however, to be the only way of validating distribution-free procedures like that of Kendall and Stuart.

J. CONCOMITANT OBSERVATIONS

The ordinary analysis of covariance is a valuable technique for eliminating the effect of factors which increase the variability within groups and perhaps distort the differences between them, but which are irrelevant to the problems being investigated. A classical application occurs in animal feeding experiments. The experimenter is concerned with the effects of diet on weight gain. He finds that weight gain is correlated with initial weight—the weight of the animals at the start of the experiment, before they had been placed on different diets. By eliminating the effect of initial weight, he is able to get a more accurate comparison of diet effects and to remove any differences between the weight gains due to chance differences in the initial weights of the animals placed on the different diets.

This is a straightforward problem that presents no difficulties of interpretation. When the concomitant observation can be affected by the treatment, matters are not so simple. Consider, as an example, the effect of a disease on wood density. Suppose that the disease reduces growth rate, and that slow growing trees have higher density in both the healthy and diseased groups. In comparing the densities of the two groups, should one take account of the rate of growth, or not? Again, in considering the effect of different diets on the size of a particular organ, should one treat total weight as a concomitant observation, or not?

Questions of this sort have nothing to do with the mathematics of the situation. They can only be answered on the basis of knowledge or assumptions about the effects of the diets or disease on the physiology of the organism.

This sort of difficulty arises very commonly in multivariate problems. Often it is hard to decide whether an observation should be included in the discriminant function, or whether it should be treated as a disturbing factor whose effect on the observations should be eliminated.

Consider again the problem of discrimination between two diseases. Suppose the age of each patient is recorded. Now there are two extreme possibilities:

(i) The two groups can be regarded as random samples from the two populations. Age is on exactly the same footing as the other observations, and it may well be that the two diseases differ in their time of onset.

(ii) Age at the time of diagnosis may well be affected by the course of the disease—for example, if diagnosis is *post mortem*, a disease which is rapidly fatal may have a lower mean age. There is therefore no evidence that the age of the patient should be regarded as a diagnostic factor. On the other hand, some of the symptoms are certainly more common among older patients with either disease, so that age must be taken into account in interpreting the symptoms.

Clearly, if (i) is true, age is to be included among the other observations in deriving the discriminant function. If, on the other hand, (ii) is true, it must be treated as a concomitant observation. Both calculations lead to a linear discriminant function involving age, but the functions are different.

In fact, as in many similar situations, the truth probably lies somewhere between these extreme assumptions. When carrying out a discriminant analysis, it is necessary to decide whether each observation is better regarded as part of the main data, or as concomitant. It is tempting to feed a mass of data into a computer without considering whether its components are logically of the same type. This temptation must be resisted, in discriminant analysis as in cluster analysis.

Once it is decided that certain observations are to be regarded as concomitant, there is no difficulty in carrying out a multivariate analysis of covariance and deriving appropriate discriminant functions. Suppose $x_1 \ldots x_k$ are concomitant, and $x_{k+1} \ldots x_p$ are the main variables. Carry out a multivariate analysis of variance of all variates to derive $p \times p$ matrices $\mathbf{W}$ and $\mathbf{S}$ for "within groups" and "total". Next form the reduced matrices $(p - k) \times (p - k)$ matrices $\mathbf{W}^*$ and $\mathbf{S}^*$ by eliminating $x_1 \ldots x_k$. The procedure is described in Appendix A Section E; the elements of $\mathbf{W}^*$ and $\mathbf{S}^*$ are simply the residual sums of squares and products after carrying out a regression on $x_1 \ldots x_k$. The degrees of freedom associated with $\mathbf{W}^*$ and $\mathbf{S}^*$ are $n - g - k$ and $n - k - 1$. The analysis on the $p - k$ adjusted variates then proceeds exactly in the usual way.

K. DISCRIMINATION WITH MORE THAN TWO GROUPS

The extension of discriminant theory to more than two groups presents no great difficulties. All the complications of the preceding sections, discussed, for simplicity for the two group case, generalize in a fairly obvious way.

The first step is to carry out a multivariate analysis of variance, as in Section C. The F test for an analysis of variance is replaced by the test based on Wilks' criterion; see Chapter 4. In this case, $L = |\mathbf{W}| / |\mathbf{S}|$, with q replaced by $g - 1$. This tests whether there is evidence of differences among the groups, and so whether any discrimination is possible.

If the L test gives a significant result, or if the first canonical correlation is significant, the next step is to determine an allocation rule. There are two ways of proceeding here. One possibility is to consider the groups in pairs, and estimate the discriminant function between each pair. The alternative is to consider the functions that maximize the variance ratio, or the variability among the groups considered together. These are the canonical variables of Chapter 4, though usually they are standardized on the matrix $\mathbf{W}$, so that they have unit variance within groups.

Both functions can be considered, in a sense, as generalizations of the discriminant function for two groups. The two approaches lead, in general, to slightly different answers, but only because the elimination of non-significant factors is carried out at different stages. The choice between the two is largely a matter of convenience.

In the first approach, the discriminant function between any two groups is calculated from the means and the pooled dispersion matrix **W**. The generalized distance can be estimated and tested, irrelevant variates discarded from the discriminant function, and an allocation rule formulated as usual. If the distances between all pairs are significant, there are $\frac{1}{2}g(g-1)$ discriminant functions.

The alternative method is to start by a canonical analysis. The latent roots of $\mathbf{WS}^{-1}$ are the squared canonical correlations of Chapter 4. If the first k are significant, and the value of $L^* = (1 - l_{k+1}) \ldots (1 - l_{g-1})$ is not significant, the first k canonical variates only are used. Original variates which are irrelevant may be discarded from them, and they are then used to derive allocation rules as in the first method. (The D^2 statistics, of course, are still regarded as based on p variates—the canonical variates have been selected to maximize the distances.)

The two methods are not in contradiction. It is possible that a distance judged just significant by the first will be just not significant by the second, and the discriminant functions will have slightly different coefficients unless all the canonical variates are used. Which approach is chosen depends essentially on whether the canonical variates give a worthwhile simplification. If $k=1$, a single discriminant function is sufficient for all the groups, and the allocation rule is simply based on a dissection of the range of this function. If $k = 2$, a scatter diagram, based with the two canonical variates as axes can be drawn to show all the groups and the lines dividing them, based on discriminant functions which are linear functions of the two canonical variates. If $k = 3$, a three-dimensional model is needed to present the data.

When $k > 3$, the advantage of using canonical variates is very slight. If g is very large, there may be some simplification, but in this case it may be better to consider doing several separate analyses.

6
Factor Analysis

A. BASIC CONCEPTS

Factor analysis is the oldest of the main multivariate techniques. The fundamental idea was suggested by Spearman (1904). It was proposed as a model for a well-defined problem in educational psychology, and it still finds most of its applications in the psychological field. Other applications have been suggested, but the model is intuitively more convincing in its original form, and it is easier to introduce it in connexion with the original application.

Suppose n students all take p different examinations. Usually, it will be found that the results are correlated; the brighter students tend to do well in all the examinations, and the less bright to do badly in all. To explain this situation, Spearman introduced the concept of "general intelligence", and suggested the model:

$$x_{ij} = a_i g_j + e_{ij}, i = 1 \ldots p, j = 1 \ldots n. \tag{1}$$

Here, x_{ij} represents the score of the jth student on the ith examination, g_j is the general intelligence of the jth student, a_i is a weighting coefficient representing the extent to which intelligence determines performance in the ith examination, and the residuals e_{ij} are uncorrelated random variables. It is generally assumed further that g is normally distributed, and that the residuals e_{ij} are independently normally distributed. Usually the x's are scaled to have unit variance; it is easily seen that the structure of the model depends only on the correlations between the x's. Obviously, the assumption that g and e are normally distributed implies also that x is normally distributed.

This model has one immediate consequence. Suppose for two examinations $i = 1,2$ the correlation between the students' scores is r_{12}. It is easily seen that the population correlation, on the basis of the model (1) is $a_1 a_2$ var g. Consequently, for any four examinations, the quantities $r_{12}r_{34} - r_{13}r_{24}$, $r_{12}r_{34} - r_{14}r_{23}$, $r_{13}r_{24} - r_{14}r_{23}$, should all be estimates of combinations of the parent correlations that are zero.

These *tetrad differences* thus provide a test of the model, and in early work on factor analysis they were widely used in this way.

Soon after the introduction of Spearman's original one-factor model, various other psychologists criticized it on the grounds that it was unrealistic, and too restrictive. Why should there not be other factors, not merely "general intelligence" but specific abilities that entered into some of the examinations but not others? These criticisms were supported by examples in which the tetrad differences were clearly different from zero, and eventually led to the formulation of an alternative multiple factor model of the form:

$$x_{ij} = \sum_{k=1}^{m} a_{ik}g_{jk} + e_{ij} \qquad (2)$$

This model involves m distinct factors. The quantities a_{ik} are known as the *factor loadings* of the different factors in the different examinations. The factors, as well as general intelligence, might include speed, linguistic ability, memory, and so on.

This is the model that defines factor analysis in the classical sense as a separate technique. The same assumptions about normality and independence are made, and the single factor model is a special case when $m = 1$. When $m \neq 1$, the tetrad differences are not zero, but any particular value of m implies some other, more complex, relationship between the correlations. Of course, m must be less than p, or the model becomes meaningless. In fact, as will be seen later, much more stringent restrictions on the value of p are necessary if estimation is to be possible.

For more than 30 years, the literature of factor analysis was largely concerned with quarrels between the supporters of the original one-factor model, and those of the multiple-factor formulation. Remarkably little was achieved on the mathematical side, and the estimation problem was tackled by methods that were, at best, crude approximations, and that lacked even the merit of objectivity and consistency—two workers believing they were using the same procedure could reach quite different conclusions. Single-factor analysis was used in the development of "intelligence tests"; among a group of tests giving more or less consistently zero tetrad differences, the best ones for estimating general intelligence are those with the largest loadings—always assuming that such a thing as general intelligence exists. The multiple-factor analysts concerned themselves chiefly with the problems of reification, and so started fresh disputes among themselves. Among mathematicians, factor analysis acquired a bad reputation, and was largely ignored.

At last, Bartlett (1938) discussed the problem from the mathematical standpoint. His proposal was essentially to estimate factor loadings from a principal components analysis of the correlation matrix. Lawley (1940) chose a different approach; assuming the model of (2), he found the maximum likelihood estimates of the factor loadings and the residual variances.

B. THE ESTIMATION PROBLEM: LAWLEY'S METHOD

The model of eqn (2) presents interesting and unusual estimation problems. In the first place, it is clearly indeterminate, and the indeterminacy is of two sorts; a change of scale in a factor g with a corresponding change in a will not affect the model, so that some form of standardization is necessary, but, except in the single-factor case $m = 1$, indeterminacy remains. If a set of factors $g_1 \ldots g_m$ are replaced by linear combinations, then the model will be completely unchanged if the coefficients of the g's in eqn (2) are unaltered. In matrix terms, eqn (2) may be written $\mathbf{x} = \mathbf{Ag} + \mathbf{e}$, and replacing $\mathbf{g}$ by $\mathbf{Bg}$ leaves the equation unchanged if $\mathbf{ABg} = \mathbf{Ag}$. There are infinitely many matrices $\mathbf{B}$ that satisfy this condition, and there is no reason for choosing any particular one, at least on mathematical grounds. This is what is meant by *factor rotation*. The usual way of tackling the estimation problem is to impose arbitrary restrictions on the factors that give a unique set, which may then be rotated for purposes of reification.

Lawley's approach to the model of eqn (2) is to estimate the coefficients a and the variances of the residuals e by maximum likelihood, assuming normal distributions for g and e, and imposing conditions that make the solution unique. Notice that the individual values of g are not estimated; if they were, the number of parameters involved would increase indefinitely with the sample size, and this means that the estimation theory breaks down completely.

Suppose that var $g_k = 1$, var $e_{ij} = \sigma_{ij}^2$. Then it is easy to see that

$$\text{var } x_i = \sum_k a_{ik}^2 + \sigma_i^2, \text{ cov } x_i x_j = \sum_k a_{ik} a_{jk}.$$

Now impose the condition

$$\sum_{t=1}^{p} a_{tj} a_{tk} / \sigma_t^2 = 0.$$

This is the condition that chooses one of the possible sets of g's that could be obtained by rotation; it is mathematically convenient, and is used merely for that reason.

Now there are $\frac{1}{2}p\,(p + 1)$ variances and covariances among the x's, and the parameters to be estimated are mp values of the a's, and p variances of the e's. The last condition imposes $\frac{1}{2}m(m - 1)$ constraints, so that the problem is indeterminate if

$$\tfrac{1}{2}p\,(p + 1) < p\,(m + 1) - \tfrac{1}{2}m\,(m - 1), \text{ or } (p - m)^2 < p + m.$$

This imposes an upper limit on the number of factors that can be fitted for a given number of tests, p. In fact, $m \leqslant p - \frac{1}{2}(\sqrt{8p + 1} - 1)$. If this condition is satisfied, there are more equations than unknowns, and estimation by maximum likelihood is possible.

The mathematics is quite difficult (for details see Lawley and Maxwell, 1963, 1970; or Kendall and Stuart, 1968) but lead eventually to a fairly simple matrix equation, which may be written

$$\hat{\mathbf{J}}\hat{\mathbf{A}}' = \hat{\mathbf{A}}'\hat{\Sigma}^{-1}\,(\mathbf{S} - \hat{\Sigma}).$$

In this equation, $\hat{\mathbf{A}}'$ is the $m \times p$ matrix of estimates of the coefficients a, $\hat{\Sigma}$ is the $m \times m$ diagonal matrix of estimates of variance of the e's, and $\hat{\mathbf{J}}$ is the $m \times m$ matrix $\hat{\mathbf{A}}'\hat{\Sigma}^{-1}\hat{\mathbf{A}}$, which is a diagonal matrix in virtue of the conditions imposed on the a's.

These equations present a difficult problem in numerical analysis. Lawley and Maxwell (1963) suggested an iterative method of solution, but later work showed that convergence was often extremely slow, and might fail altogether. In the second edition (Lawley and Maxwell, 1970) they proposed a completely different iterative method, which they claim to have much more satisfactory convergence properties.

The maximum likelihood method leads to a significance test, based on the variances and covariances of the x's, and the estimates of these quantities from the estimates of the a's and the variances of the e's. If $\mathbf{S}$ is the sample dispersion matrix, and $\mathbf{S}^* = \hat{\mathbf{A}}\hat{\mathbf{A}}' + \hat{\Sigma}$, the quantity $-n \ln |\mathbf{S}| / |\mathbf{S}^*| - \text{tr}(\mathbf{SS}^{*-1}) + p$ is approximately distributed as χ^2 with $\frac{1}{2}\{(p - m)^2 - (p + m)\}$ d.f. A better approximation (Bartlett, 1951) is given by replacing n by

$$n - \frac{(2p + 11 - 4m)}{6}.$$

The procedure, then, is to fit a single factor and test significance. If the value of χ^2 is not significant, a single-factor model explains the results satisfactorily; if it is significant, fit two factors and test again, and so on until the model is found that gives a satisfactory fit with the minimum number of factors. It is possible that no admissible value of m gives a satisfactory fit. In this case, the problem cannot be solved.

C. PRINCIPAL COMPONENTS AND FACTOR ANALYSIS

It is clear that the sort of structure underlying the factor analysis problem must be disentangled by considering the correlations between the x's. Now, one way of extracting the most important factors in this situation is to carry out a principal component analysis on the correlation matrix—a principal component analysis standardizing the variances. This is a much simpler procedure than the maximum likelihood method, and it is not obvious how the two approaches differ.

In fact, the model of eqn (2) would give precisely the first m principal components as the factors if, instead of using Lawley's method, one proceeded to minimize the sum of squares of the residuals. The factor-analysis approach, however, is not concerned with the magnitude of the residuals, but with the correlations between them. It is true that removing the first principal components from the correlation matrix does usually greatly reduce the correlations among the residuals, and in this sense principal component analysis can be regarded as an approximation to factor analysis. Nevertheless, regarding eqn (2) as a definite model, in which the relationship among the x's is explained by precisely m factors, and the residuals are therefore uncorrelated, principal component analysis is not an attempt to fit the model.

The distinction, then, is that a factor analysis with m factors assumes a very definite mathematical model, whereas principal component analysis does not. A principal component analysis picks out the m most important factors, without necessarily assuming that the residuals are completely uncorrelated or that they are normally distributed. Bartlett's test for the remaining $p - m$ latent roots then tests whether the residuals are independent, and so whether the roots are distinguishable —whether there is any point in trying to extract further factors.

The critical point in deciding whether to do a factor analysis is the validity of the factor model. Some authors feel that even in the psychological situation for which it was designed the factor model is unrealistic (Rao, 1965). Others (Lawley and Maxwell, 1970) suggest that it has many applications outside this field.

D. OTHER FACTOR MODELS

In factor analysis, the probability that certain observed variables take certain values is related to the values of a smaller number of postulated variables. In classical factor analysis, as has already been described, the factors and the observed variates are assumed to be normally distributed, and the relationship determines the mean of the latter. It is possible to postulate different sorts of relationship, equally strictly defined, between the variates and the factors.

In particular, factor analysis models have been suggested for the situation when the variates are binary. The binary variates may be related to factors assumed normally distributed (Anderson, 1974) or to assumed binary factors (Lazarsfeld and Henry, 1968). In the latter case, the binary factors can be regarded as defining a grouping of the observations. This model is further considered in Chapter 8, under cluster analysis.

E. REIFICATION

The general discussion of reification in principal component analysis (Chapter 4) applies equally to reification in factor analysis, but there are a few further points.

In the first place, there is absolutely no reason why the factors derived by Lawley's technique should have any meaning. Rotation, which is only occasionally worth considering in principal component analysis, is in factor analysis almost always an essential preliminary to reification. The factors derived by Lawley's method are uncorrelated; there is no reason why the combinations used for reification should be so.

Secondly, many psychologists feel that, in the original psychological application, the coefficients of a factor, to be identified as a specific ability, should have certain constraints; in particular, negative factor loadings, implying that a specific ability adversely affects performance in a particular test, are often felt to be unrealistic. This has lead to methods for estimating factors subject to certain constraints (Lawley and Maxwell, 1970).

The idea of "general intelligence" and "specific abilities" still attracts psychologists, and this suggests that the easiest factor structure to reify will be one in which the first factor has positive loadings in all tests, and the others have mainly zero loadings and enter into only a small group of tests. This is the idea behind "simple structure" methods of reification (Thurstone, 1947). There is some analogy with the concept of "size" and "shape" (Chapter 4).

These special considerations, however, apply, for the most part, only to the original psychological problem. Again, reification has little connexion with the mathematics; the experimenter is free to manipulate the factors as he likes, and to interpret them in the way he thinks most reasonable in the experimental situation.

F. APPLICATIONS

In its original context, factor analysis has been widely used, and has provided useful insights into the factors that enter into various tests, and some practical guidance in such problems as the construction of "intelligence tests" with particular properties. A few critics of the method have suggested that the factor model is unrealistic, and that other techniques, especially principal component analysis, distort the true situation less. This is perhaps a less serious criticism than it might appear; factor analysis includes a significance test, and if the test indicates that the fit is satisfactory, probably other methods would give much the same result (Gower, 1967). If the critics are right, the more difficult calculations are probably a waste of time, but are unlikely to be misleading.

Perhaps a more interesting question is whether the factor model is likely to prove useful in other contexts. The critical assumptions in eqn (2) are that there are precisely m factors, that factors and residuals are normally distributed, and that the relationship is linear. The last assumption is perhaps the most important; like the assumption of linearity in many other statistical applications, it is likely to be a reasonable approximation if the range of the variables is fairly small, but not to work well for extreme values. In psychological applications this condition is usually fulfilled. Nobody is likely to give the same tests, for example, to a group containing young children and intelligent adults and expect the results to conform to the factor analysis model. Similarly, it may be reasonable to say that the result of a test depends linearly on general intelligence and graphical ability, but nobody could expect a reliable prediction for an imaginary examinee with enormous intelligence but extremely low graphical ability.

It is probably the breakdown of linearity for extreme values that most limits the plausibility of the factor model in other situations. Blackith and Reyment (1971) discussed some half-dozen cases in which factor analysis has been used in biology, geology, and ecological studies; they concluded: "We have yet to discover any illustration of the superiority of factor analysis over principal components analysis." It is hard to disagree with this, at least as far as the classical form of factor analysis defined by eqn (2) is concerned.

7

Distance, Similarity and Scaling

A. DISTANCE AS A MEASURE OF DISSIMILARITY

If the coordinates in a p-dimensional scatter diagram represent the values of p variables measured on N individuals, it is obvious, in general terms, that points that are very close together represent individuals that are similar in these characters, while points that are far apart represent individuals that are dissimilar. Thus distance in a diagram of this sort is a measure of dissimilarity.

The ordinary distance between two points $(x_1 \ldots x_p)$ and $(x_1{}^* \ldots x_p{}^*)$, sometimes called the Euclidean distance, is given by

$$D^2 = (x_1 - x_1{}^*)^2 + \ldots (x_p - x_p{}^*)^2.$$

This measure of course depends on the scale of the variables. It is unlikely to have much meaning as a measure of dissimilarity if some variables have a much greater range of values than others. Accordingly, the Euclidean distance is usually used as a measure of dissimilarity only when all the measurements are of the same type, or when they have been standardized in some way.

The experimenter may feel, however, that some of the variables recorded are much more important than others in deciding whether two individuals are similar. A botanist, for example, may feel that in the taxonomy of plants the structure of the flowers is more important than their colour or than the height of the plant. He may feel that a weighted distance, given by

$$D^2 = k_1(x_1 - x_1{}^*)^2 + \ldots k_p(x_p - x_p{}^*)^2$$

in which $k_1 \ldots k_p$ are weights based on his idea of the relative importance of the characters, is a better measure of dissimilarity.

In some cases, the Euclidean distance is a very unsatisfactory measure of dissimilarity. Suppose the measurements are all lengths. The distance between two points will then reflect, more than anything else, differences

51

in size (cf. Chapter 4), which are generally of little interest to the morphologist. Here the direction of the point from the origin, rather than its distance, is an indication of shape, and a better measure of dissimilarity might be related to the angle between these directions. For points $\mathbf{x}$ and $\mathbf{x}^*$, this is given by

$$\cos^2 \theta = \frac{(\Sigma\, x_i x_i^*)^2}{\Sigma\, x_i^2\, \Sigma\, x_i^{*2}}$$

Notice the relationship between this measure and the correlation coefficient. Cos θ is, in fact, the correlation, taken from the origin, not the mean, of the two sets of coordinates treated as if they were two samples of p variates.

A more subtle use of angles as measures of dissimilarity occurs when one is considering the similarity of *response* to a change or a difference of some sort. This response can be represented by a line with a certain direction, and the angle between two directions is a measure of dissimilarity of response. Blackith (1962) used this technique to analyse the response of different species of locust to crowding, and Reyment (1969) discussed its application to sex differences (for details, see Blackith and Reyment, 1971).

When the measurements are log lengths, a more logical measure of dissimilarity is the sum of squares of differences *taken from the mean difference*, or $\Sigma(x_i - x_i^* - d)^2$, where d is the mean difference,

$$d = \frac{1}{p} \Sigma(x_i - x_i^*).$$

This quantity is proportional to the variance of the differences regarded as a sample; it is zero if the original lengths are all proportional, and so is independent of size.

Another problem concerns the use of highly correlated variates in defining a measure of dissimilarity. The effect of including logically correlated measures, such as, say, length, girth, and weight, all of which reflect differences in size, is to increase the emphasis given to the character. There is thus a case for reducing the weight given to correlated characters. On the other hand, there is a real risk of discarding valuable information by doing so. If it is found that in a human population height, hair colour, eye colour, and skin pigmentation are correlated, it may well imply the existence of two races, one tall and fair, the other short and dark. Gower (1969) made this point.

There is a real difficulty here, and a real conflict of opinion. It is easy to say that logically correlated characters should be excluded, or given smaller weights, while correlations that could not have been predicted should be ignored, but it is often difficult to decide what are logically correlated variates. Sokal (1961) regarded the use of the Euclidean distance as a more "natural" measure of dissimilarity, while other authors are inclined to eliminate correlations, using Mahalanobis' generalized distance, or some related measure.

Mahalanobis' generalized distance was originally defined as the generalized distance between the means of two groups, based on the dispersion matrix *within* groups (see Chapter 5). It is logical to extend the definition to give the generalized distance between any two points in this situation. It is much less logical to extend it further to the case where there is only one group. In particular, if the distance measure is to be used to determine a grouping, it is illogical to eliminate the correlations *before* the grouping is formed.

The use of Mahalanobis' generalized distance in cluster analysis in the way described by Friedman and Rubin (1967) or Marriott (1971), effectively *after* the grouping is formed, is perfectly reasonable (see Chapter 8), but there seems little justification for its use when there is no existing subdivision. On the other hand, the arguments for using equal weights (an "unweighted" distance measure, as it is sometimes misleadingly called) are equally tenuous, and give a measure that is very sensitive to the characters chosen for analysis.

In fact, there is no mathematical or logical justification for any particular system of weighting. A measure of dissimilarity is essentially a subjective measure, and the experimenter must take the responsibility for deciding what characters to include, and what weights to give them. The decision cannot be shuffled on to the shoulders of the mathematicians.

All this discussion shows that in some situations the Euclidean distance is a reasonable measure of dissimilarity, while in others it is not. The inverse problem, of representing graphically dissimilarity measures by distances, presents no such difficulties. An isometric chart, in which the distances do represent an accepted measure of dissimilarity, is a useful tool with no logical complications. It is with this inverse problem that the remainder of this chapter will be mainly concerned.

B. SIMILARITY AND DISSIMILARITY MEASURES

Sometimes, rather than specifying the values of a set of characters, it is more convenient to work from the start with measures of similarity or dissimilarity. It may be easier to give a subjective similarity score to each pair of objects than to record values of variates. Again, if variates are recorded, the experimenter may feel that he has more confidence in a similarity measure based on the variates than on the recorded values.

This may be so, for example, when there are many missing values, or when the distribution of the variates is awkward and cannot easily be made more satisfactory by a transformation. For a fuller discussion of similarity measures based on variates, see Jardine and Sibson (1970) and Blackith and Reyment (1971).

A similarity measure may be defined as a non-negative quantity that increases with the similarity between the two individuals concerned. The similarity measure between A and B may be written $s(AB)$. In the same way, a dissimilarity measure $d(AB)$ is a non-negative measure that decreases as $s(AB)$ increases. Thus $1/s(AB)$ and $C - s(AB)$, where C is not less than any value of $s(AB)$, are possible dissimilarity measures.

If a dissimilarity measure is to be regarded as a distance, it must also have the metric property, $d(AB) \leqslant d(AC) + d(BC)$, for any three items A, B, and C. Sibson (1972) emphasized that this is by no means a necessary property of a measure of dissimilarity, and claims that non-metric measures of dissimilarity have many advantages. Certainly they can be used without difficulty in the construction of dendrograms. Nevertheless, the possibility of other types of graphical presentation is such an important feature in interpreting the results that I feel that a metric dissimilarity measure that can be interpreted as a distance has overriding advantages in most situations.

Once such a distance measure has been defined, it is easy to derive a set of coordinates for each point that have the required set of $\frac{1}{2}N(N-1)$ distances, but in general it requires $N - 1$ dimensions. A possible algorithm for doing so would be to place the first point at the origin, the second at the appropriate distance along the axis of x_1, the third in the $x_1 x_2$ plane at the assigned distance from the other two, and so on. The addition of each new point involves the introduction of a new coordinate, and the placing of the mth point involves the solution of $m - 1$ equations in $m - 1$ unknowns. There remains one ambiguity, which can be resolved by specifying that the $(m - 1)$th coordinate of the mth point shall be positive (otherwise the fourth point, for example, could be placed above or below the plane of the first three).

A rule of this sort makes it possible to transform the $\frac{1}{2}N(N-1)$ distances into a set of coordinates. It is unambiguous, in the sense that the shape of the resulting configuration is completely determined. A different algorithm might produce quite a different coordinate system, but the structure, apart from rotations and reflections, would remain the same. This sort of transformation is, of course, quite impossible if the metric property is not satisfied.

As an example of a distance measure, suppose a series of bacterial cultures are subjected to a battery of twenty tests. A reasonable index of similarity is the number of tests to which both items give a positive response; cases in which only one gives a positive response, and cases in which both give negative responses, are both scored zero. Thus a similarity index is defined, ranging from 0 to 20. As a dissimilarity measure, $1/s$ (or, to avoid the infinite value, $1/(s + 1)$), could be used, but it is easy to see that they do not satisfy the metric inequality; consider, for example, $s(AB) = 8$, $s(AC) = 9$, $s(BC) = 0$). On the other hand, $20 - s$ is a dissimilarity measure that does satisfy the metric inequality.

C. MULTIDIMENSIONAL SCALING

The fact that a strict representation of the set of $\frac{1}{2}N(N - 1)$ distances between N items in coordinate form requires $N - 1$ dimensions is rather a serious drawback. Often N is large, in most applications of ordinary multivariate techniques much larger than p, the number of variates, and handling N-dimensional matrices can tax even a powerful computer. It is therefore worth considering whether it is possible to represent the distances approximately, without too much distortion, in a space of many fewer dimensions.

To approach the same problem from a rather different point of view, suppose the data are the distances between N points known to lie in p dimensions, but there are considerable errors in the measurements; they might, for example, be some indirect measure of distance like the train times between towns. The problem now is to reconstruct, as accurately as possible, the original p-dimensional structure.

A third possibility is that the value of p is unknown, and the aim is to find the smallest value of p that seems consistent with the idea that the original distances were measured in p dimensions and were subject to random errors. The next step is then to reconstruct the p-dimensional arrangement, as before.

These are all problems in reduction of dimensionality, or as it is sometimes called, ordination. This term originally meant reduction to one dimension, or ordering; it has now been extended to presentation in fewer dimensions. They could all be tackled by transforming to a coordinate system and using techniques that have already been discussed. The first and third problems are straightforward applications of principal component analysis, the second is a perfect example of factor analysis, with the number of factors known.

This indirect approach to the problem, however, presents certain difficulties. In the first place, the computation can become very heavy. It involves handling $N \times N$ matrices, and the labour involved is largely unnecessary. Secondly, since the distances are regarded as the fundamental variables, it seems more logical to look for a p-dimensional representation that optimizes a function of them, rather than work with derived coordinates. For these reasons, methods of ordination based directly on the differences have been evolved.

It is important, though, to realize that these multivariate scaling methods are not essentially different from other multivariate methods. Rather large claims have been made for the advantages of such techniques. Any advantages they have are due to the use of dissimilarity, or distance, measures rather than the original variates (if any). The techniques themselves are logically equivalent, or virtually so, to other multivariate methods, and are better only in that the computations are easier.

Various scaling methods have been devised; the principle is essentially the same in all. To place the points in p dimensions, the first $p + 1$ points are fixed at their proper distances, and the remainder added one at a time in positions that optimize their distances from those already placed. When all the points are placed, further cycles of adjustment are carried out until no further substantial improvement seems possible.

Perhaps the best known multidimensional scaling procedure is that of Shepard, further developed by Kruskal (1964). The effectiveness of the method is demonstrated by a remarkable reconstruction of the map of the *départements* of France, by Kendall (1971), based on a binary similarity measure representing "touching" or "not touching", and an idea due to E. M. Wilkinson for converting this measure to a metric one. The reproduction is certainly impressive (Fig. 7.1), but it must be admitted that the fact that the *départements* are of comparable size and form a more or less hexagonal grid over a more or less square country probably contributed to the success. An entirely different technique (not involving multidimensional scaling) has since been devised by Kendall (1972, 1974) explicitly for the solution of problems such as this, which arise in a natural way in the context of historical geography.

D. APPLICATIONS

The calculation of distances or dissimilarities is the first step in many techniques of cluster analysis. In a sense, the set of $\frac{1}{2}N(N-1)$ distances is an alternative to the set of Np coordinates as a way of describing the individuals concerned, but the relationship between the two is very close. From the coordinates, provided they satisfy the metric inequality, it is easy to derive a set of distances, either simple Euclidean distances

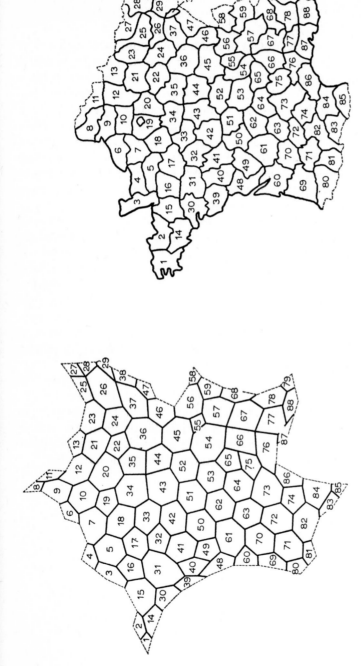

Fig. 7.1

The map of France reconstructed by D. G. Kendall's multidimensional scaling technique, compared with the real map. The reconstruction was based on a binary measure of similarity, indicating whether each pair of *départements* touched, or not. This was the only piece of data given to the computer program that made the map.

or some other measures of dissimilarity satisfying the metric inequality. It is easy to derive from the distances a set of coordinates with Euclidean distances approximately equal to those given. In fact, the distances can be regarded as a transformation of the coordinates.

It follows that the advantages of working with distances rather than coordinates are those of a suitable transformation; it is not a question of an entirely different approach. It is often claimed that suitable distance measures are more flexible than coordinate systems, that methods based on them are less sensitive to departures from the assumptions made in coordinate-based techniques, that distances based on ranks or coarse groupings have the advantages of non-parametric statistics. These claims contain a good deal of truth, but should not be exaggerated. Choosing an appropriate distance measure is a matter requiring skill and experience, and a mere routine change from coordinates to distances confers no special advantages.

The flexibility of distance measures is really valuable when it enables the experimenter to use his judgment and knowledge of the sort of data involved. Some types of data, as has been mentioned in Chapter 1, are difficult to handle and do not lend themselves readily to simple mathematical transformations. Two examples are situations in which there are many missing values, and variables with a high probability of taking one particular value, usually zero. In such cases, the experimenter may often feel more confidence in a measure of dissimilarity, determined by his judgment, than in guesses at the missing values or at a reasonable transformation.

Many sorts of distance measures have been proposed (see, for example, Jardine and Sibson, 1971; Blackith and Reyment, 1971). There is no point in arguing about which is "best". The experimenter must choose that which seems to him best for his problem; the mathematician cannot give much guidance. It is precisely this subjective element that gives distance-based methods their particular value.

8
Cluster Analysis and Related Problems

A. INTRODUCTION

In the past ten years, there has been great activity in the study of techniques called variously cluster analysis, classification, numerical taxonomy, and dissection. The whole field is in a state of rapid development, and of considerable confusion; some of the developments have been illuminating and exciting, but at the same time there have been a number of cases of techniques misunderstood and misapplied, leading to misleading results. A survey of the whole field would be impossible, and would certainly be out of date in a year or two. This chapter will be restricted to a discussion of the general problems and principles, and an examination of some of the methods that are most popular, or seem most promising.

The problems fall into four categories, which overlap to some extent:

(i) What is the best way of dividing the individuals into a given number of groups? This type of question is called "dissection" by Kendall and Stuart (1968). There is no implication that the resulting groups are in any sense a natural division of the data; the problem is merely to find the most convenient way of dividing the sample into categories.

(ii) Is there a "natural" subdivision of the individuals into groups? This is the most interesting and important problem; it occurs in taxonomy, where species and genera can be regarded—at least in theory—as natural groups; in medicine and psychiatry, where syndromes may indicate distinct disorders; in ecology, where environmental features may lead to a number of more or less homogeneous, and distinct, categories; and in many other disciplines. This is the problem of *classification*,* or *cluster analysis*. Kendall and Stuart (1968)

---

* Classification is also sometimes used for the procedure of assigning individuals to groups with known properties, the formulation of allocation rules discussed in Chapter 5.

suggested reserving the term cluster analysis for the clustering of variables, but this suggestion does not seem to have been generally adopted.

(iii) Is there a natural subdivision of the *variables* into groups? This question has two possible applications. In the first place there are problems in theoretical statistics concerned with which variables should be retained and which discarded, and the question may throw light on them. Secondly, there is sometimes a sort of duality between what are regarded as variables and what as individuals, and a grouping of variables may have a direct experimental practical interest.

(iv) What is the best way of constructing a strictly hierarchical classification, and plotting a dendrogram, for these individuals? The meaning of these terms will become clear later. Expressing the relationship between the items in the form of a tree implies a special sort of structure. It is a process that is often confused with the search for a natural grouping, but it is really quite distinct.

This group of questions occurs in many different contexts. The questions are linked to other problems—spatial dispersion, pattern recognition, the study of time series—that are currently the subject of much research. Dozens of methods of solving them have been suggested, a whole vocabulary of technical jargon has been evolved, and yet it must be admitted that the tools available are crude, fallible, and not properly understood.

B. DISSECTION

In many situations, it is useful to subdivide a population or a sample without any implication that it is, in any sense, composite or non-homogeneous. For example, a dress manufacturer may conduct a study on his customers and divide them into size-groups, and then make dresses in sizes that correspond to these groups. A soil scientist may wish to divide soils into convenient categories, even if he believes that the soils in the area under study form a continuous series.

The best way of doing dissections of this sort is simply the most convenient: the problem is essentially a practical, not a mathematical, one. It may be useful to choose a dissection that maximizes or minimizes some function of the observations, such as the sum of squares of deviations from the group means, but the choice of such a procedure is made, and judged, on practical grounds.

The number of groups is arbitrary. The soil scientist may decide beforehand how many groups he would like; the dress manufacturer may try, on the basis of his sample, to balance the extra cost of a larger number of size groups against the possible increase in sales.

As a rule, the most convenient groups will not differ very greatly in size. Groups containing only a few individuals will often be attached to a larger group, or combined, with a gain in simplicity and little loss of information. A group containing most of the observations will often be subdivided, not because it is too heterogeneous, but because it is too cumbersome.

If there is, in fact, a natural grouping, often—but by no means necessarily—the most convenient grouping will be based on this natural grouping, perhaps subdividing the largest groups and combining some of the smaller ones. This sort of relationship between a natural grouping and a convenient one is the only real justification for the use of cluster analysis methods for dissection, and they are very commonly so used.

Dissection thus involves no mathematical theory and no mathematical difficulties. Grouping may be based on some optimization procedure, and this may present computing problems, but the only real criterion of the value of a grouping is its utility.

C. CLUSTERING OF VARIABLES

The problem of examining the clustering of variables, as opposed to individuals, has not attracted very much attention. It has been suggested as a useful approach to the still unsolved problem of selecting variables for further study in multiple regression or in multivariate procedures. Often there is considerable redundancy among the variables, and it would be useful to have reliable criteria for rejecting some and retaining others. Many suggestions have been made, but none is altogether satisfactory. A study of the clustering of the variables is at least a reasonable first step towards the decision.

A more direct application is sometimes possible. Suppose N areas of ground are studied, and the number of plants of each species in each area are recorded. If a total of p species are found, variables $x_1 \ldots x_p$ may be defined, giving the number of each of the p species (or binary variables, indicating presence or absence may be used) in each of the N areas.

The same problem may be parameterized in a different way. A variate can be allotted to each *site* and its value recorded for each of the p plants found (or for each of a precompiled list of plants). Now there are two distinct questions that may be asked:

(i) Do the plants tend to fall into groups, occurring together on the same sites?

(ii) Do the sites tend to fall into groups, having similar plant communities?

Whichever parameterization is adopted, one of these questions refers to clustering of individuals, the other to clustering of variables. This sort of duality is quite common; one may be interested in grouping patients with similar symptoms, or in grouping symptoms that tend to form syndromes. In these situations clustering of variables may be of interest in itself, and this is a separate reason for examining it.

In fact, the clustering of variables is almost the same problem as the clustering of individuals. It is natural to use the correlation between two variables as a measure of similarity, though some caution is necessary. "It must be remembered that correlation coefficients are quantities of a highly summary kind, and it is prudent, as a preliminary in all these cases to draw some of the bivariate scatter diagrams in order to get an overall view of the nature of the variation." (Kendall and Stuart, 1968) Usually the sign of the correlation coefficient is unimportant, since it is reversed by changing the sign of one of the variables, and one suitable measure of dissimilarity that obeys the metric inequality is $1 - r^2$. Using this, or any other suitable measure of dissimilarity, analysis proceeds by any of the methods used for clustering individuals.

D. NESTED GROUPINGS AND DENDROGRAMS

A nested grouping, or a strictly hierarchical grouping, is a series of subdivisions of the data into g groups, in which g varies from 1 to N, with the property that the divisions into g and $g + 1$ groups have $g - 1$ identical groups, and differ only in that the remaining items are in a single group in the first case and are divided into two in the second.

This sort of grouping is usually achieved in one of two ways:

(i) Starting from a single group containing all the items, divide it into two, according to some prescribed criterion: for example, to minimize some measure of variability within the groups. Next, subdivide one of the resulting groups, again choosing the division according to the criterion chosen. Continue the process until there are N groups each containing a single item.

(ii) Starting from N groups each containing one item, combine the two nearest items. Next, combine the two nearest groups—either joining two single items, or attaching a third item to the group of two already formed. Continue the process until all the items are included in a single group. Naturally, the criterion of "nearness" can be defined in various ways, and in general these will lead to different groupings.

These methods are called respectively *divisive* and *agglomerative*. It is worth emphasizing that it is the algorithm, rather than the solution, that is divisive or agglomerative. The same method can sometimes be programmed in either way, though as a rule one or other will be much simpler. It is thus rather illogical to discuss the advantages of the two approaches as if they were distinct solutions.

In practice, the divisive method presents impossible computational difficulties unless N is very small. There are $2^{(N-1)} - 1$ ways of making the first subdivision, and to compute a statistic for each of them and choose the optimum quickly becomes a task beyond the capability of even a powerful computer. Edwards and Cavalli-Sforza (1965) discuss the method; they conclude that an upper limit of about $N = 16$ is practicable. A different approach, starting from a plausible guess and improving the solution by moving items from one group to another, is more hopeful (Rubin, 1967), but there is no guarantee that the unique optimum solution will be reached.

The agglomerative method, on the other hand, is usually easy to compute, and may even not require the construction of a computer program. An example of the simplest type of agglomerative procedure is illustrated in Fig. 8.1. The order in which the links are joined up depends only on the distances between the points.

The simple process of Fig. 8.1 is known as single-link clustering. It may be modified in various ways, apart from the obvious one of using

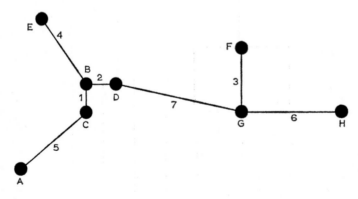

FIG. 8.1

Simple nearest-neighbour single-link agglomerative clustering. The points A–H are shown on a scatter diagram. Links are formed in the order shown. First, B and C, the closest pair of points, are joined. Next, BD, and then FG are formed. The distance CD is actually less than FG, but C and D are already linked by the path CBD, so this link is ignored. The process is continued by joining BE, CA, GH, and DG, until all the points are linked together.

a different distance metric. The distance between *groups* can be defined differently, for example, as the distance between their centroids. This may often seem more logical, but it involves certain difficulties; in particular, if two distances happen to be equal, the order in which the links are made affects the subsequent grouping.

When the nested grouping has been carried out, it can be represented graphically by a dendrogram. A dendrogram is a tree diagram in which the extremities (usually shown at the bottom) represent the individuals, and the branching of the tree gives the order of joining together. Thus working from the bottom line, the first fork represents the first link, the second fork the second link, and so on until all join together at the trunk. Alternatively, in a divisive system, the first fork from the trunk represents the first division, and so on. Figure 8.2 gives the dendrogram corresponding to the linkage in Fig. 8.1.

There is one feature common to most agglomerative methods: a link once made can never be broken, and a chain joining two compact groups prevents their ever being separated. The point is illustrated in Fig. 8.3. In two-dimensional space, a chance linking of two natural groups in this way is rather unlikely; in space of higher dimensionality the risk is much greater. This possibility of chaining is usually regarded as a defect of the method, but if the purpose of the analysis is to investi-

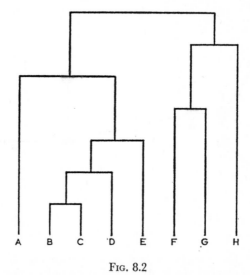

FIG. 8.2

A dendrogram for the data of Fig. 8.1. The level of the horizontal lines shows the order in which the links were formed; thus, the first link joins B and C, the second joins D to B and C, the third joins E to B, C and D, and so on. The final link joins the groups ABCDE and FGH.

gate the relationship between the items, rather than to look for natural groups, the existence of the intermediate points may be an important indication that items apparently very different are in fact related.

It is possible, in fact, to construct a mathematical model for which single-linkage clustering is an optimum solution. Suppose the data consist of binary observations, and suppose each variate represents a single feature of the individual concerned. Suppose that evolution proceeds by spontaneous changes in these features. (In the biological context, it is natural to think in terms of genes and mutations, but conceivably such a model might apply to other situations, for example to the development of archeological artifacts.) Suppose further that the chance of such a change occurring twice, or reversing, is negligible. Then the problem of reconstructing the evolutionary history is closely related to that of forming a tree in which the proximity of the apices depends only on the number of features they have in common (Hartigan, 1973).

There are many variations of nested, hierarchical techniques, but they all have in common the structural features associated with the dendrogram. These common features are perhaps more important than the details of the procedure.

Nested structures are of interest to the mathematician; they have the structure of "trees", which are studied in graph theory, an important branch of abstract algebra. Consequently, their properties are fairly

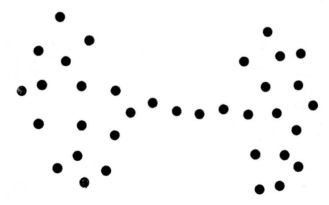

Fig. 8.3

Here there are fairly clearly two clusters, and most divisive methods of cluster analysis would detect them easily. Most agglomerative hierarchical methods, however, would join up the chain between them at an early stage in the process, and it could never be broken thereafter.

This sort of chaining is rather unlikely to occur in such an extreme form in a two-dimensional situation. With more variates, the risk is increased.

well known, and their practical application is attractive to the pure algebraist. The taxonomist is also familiar with the tree structure; identification trees are well known, particularly in botany, and "family trees" illustrating the course of evolution are commonly used. Finally, the problems of numerical analysis are fairly simple for the agglomerative procedures, and often a computer program is not even necessary.

These are the features that account for the popularity of strictly hierarchical techniques. There remains, however the critical question: What is the aim of the analysis, and what does the dendrogram represent when it has been constructed?

Hartigan's (1973) example gives a possible answer; it may be an attempt to reconstruct the course of evolution. At the same time, the example illustrates the difficulties of this approach. The proposed model of the evolutionary process is so much simplified that it is unrealistic in any biological context, and probably in any other. In fact, users of these techniques do not claim to be reconstructing an evolutionary tree. They seem rather to be trying to group the data in natural classes, and to illustrate this grouping by the dendrogram.

As a method of cluster analysis, if there is no special reason for imposing the nested structure of the dendrogram, the strictly hierarchical methods have serious disadvantages. It is true that if there is a clear, unambiguous grouping, with little or no overlap between the groups, any method will reach this grouping, but the hierarchical techniques are not primarily adapted to finding groups. If a division into two groups is optimum, the subsequent division into three is most unlikely to be so. The restriction that one of the groups is the same in both cases is not a natural one to impose if the purpose is to find a natural grouping. Further, it makes a comparison of divisions into different numbers of groups extremely difficult. To decide whether a division into two or three groups gives a better representation of the data, it is necessary to compare the best division into two with the best division into three, and hierarchical methods will not usually give both.

Blackith and Reyment (1971) concluded: "It seems likely that hierarchical techniques are almost always undesirable in theory . . ." They modified this conclusion by adding that in practice the consequences may not be serious. The latter argument is hard to accept. If the hierarchical structure is inappropriate, there is no reason to impose it. There are many alternative approaches that are no harder to apply, that will detect an obvious grouping quite as well, and that make it much easier to decide when a good grouping has been found.

If the aim of the analysis is merely to find an appropriate grouping, the imposition of a hierarchical structure is pointless. There is therefore little point in comparing different types of hierarchical methods, and it is better to consider the clustering problem *ab initio*, without imposing any conditions.

E. CLASSIFICATION, OR CLUSTER ANALYSIS

1. General considerations

Classification, or cluster analysis, has been defined as the search for a natural grouping, but so far no attempt has been made to define what is meant by a natural grouping. It seems reasonable to associate a natural grouping with multimodality; few people would agree that a distribution with a single mode consists of more than one "natural" group, but if there is clear evidence of clustering round several modes, it would be fairly generally accepted that there is evidence of several groups.

This approach, however, involves several difficulties. In the first place, the data must be regarded as a random sample from a population. As has already been mentioned, this assumption is not always reasonable. The items may, in fact, consist of all existing species in a class, or they may constitute a sample, but a selected sample, from a population. This difficulty will be ignored, because multimodality is impossible to define, at least for continuous measurements, unless the assumption is made.

Secondly, multimodality of a theoretical distribution is not always easy to define. For a continuous multivariate distribution there is no problem. For binary variates, again it is easy to frame a logical definition in terms of paths moving away from the vertex of maximum concentration. With grouped data, and especially with mixtures of continuous and discrete variates, there are real difficulties. The only possible approach seems to be to assume that the discrete variates represent a grouping of some underlying continuous variate.

Assumptions of this sort make it possible to define a natural grouping in terms of a sample that gives evidence of being drawn from a multimodal distribution. Thus the problem of cluster analysis becomes that of detecting, with some sort of significance test, an underlying multimodality, and then finding an allocation rule for assigning the items to the groups thus defined. A procedure of this sort should be invariant under linear transformations, though not, of course, under all transformations.

The problem of concomitant observations is much clearer in the case of cluster analysis than in that of discriminant analysis. The problem is to find a natural grouping, but obviously one is not necessarily looking for any natural grouping. A simple example is provided by sex. In a medical investigation where the purpose is to decide whether a group of patients are suffering from a single, homogeneous disorder, or from a group of related, but distinct, diseases, obviously the inclusion of male and female patients creates difficulties. There is, unquestionably, a natural grouping, but clearly it would be absurd to divide the patients, by some form of cluster analysis, into groups primarily on the basis of their sex. There is a very real risk that this will happen, and for the purposes of the analysis either the two sexes must be considered separately, or sex must be treated as a concomitant variable, and somehow its effect must be eliminated.

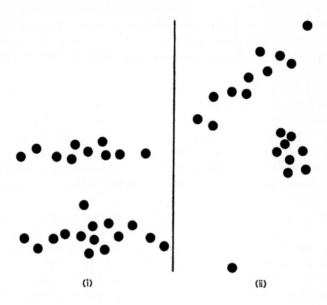

(i)   (ii)

FIG. 8.4

Many methods of cluster analysis break down for particular types of cluster that are, nevertheless, obvious to the eye.

(i) Elongated clusters are not easily detected by methods based on simple Euclidean distance. This sort of situation is not well suited to Wishart's modal analysis, nor to methods that minimize $\text{tr}(\mathbf{W})$, the sum of the variances within groups.

Standardization of variates to the same standard deviation may help, but the case when the variates are correlated and the clustering corresponds to some combination of them is still awkward.

(ii) Here there are two clusters with very different dispersion matrices, and an outlier. Techniques that assume, explicitly or implicitly, the same dispersion matrices within clusters, are inefficient in such situations. Many methods tend to give clusters of approximately equal size, and failure to detect and eliminate an outlier can distort the procedure.

2. The use of principal components

The value of a graphical examination of the data has already been mentioned. The most usual approach is to plot principal components, in pairs or possibly in more than two dimensions, and examine the scatter diagrams. Often a grouping is obvious to the eye that is less easy to detect using numerical methods of cluster analysis. Figure 8.4 illustrates some cases in which at least certain methods of cluster analysis might give misleading results, but where the groups are obvious from the graphs.

Perhaps even more important, an examination of the graphs can confirm or cast doubt on the existence of a grouping produced by numerical methods. Few classification techniques include a test of significance, and a grouping that is not obvious from a careful examination of the principal components may well be spurious.

There has been some discussion about the relative merits of classification procedures and ordination methods, as if they were alternative treatments of the problem. In fact, they are complementary. A division into groups may be an inappropriate way of summarizing the results; if so, both ordination and cluster analysis should indicate this conclusion. If there is no natural subdivision, ordination may still throw some light on the relationship between the observations. If there is, both methods should indicate it. There is certainly no conflict between the two, in aims at least. If they appear to give different results, one is wrong. Either the ordination has not been examined sufficiently critically, or the clustering method used has met a problem for which it is not well suited.

3. Mixtures of normal distributions: Day's method

The problem of estimating the parameters of a mixture of (univariate) normal distributions is an extremely unpleasant one. It was studied by Karl Pearson, whose solution was based on the moments of the combined distribution, and anyone who has tried to use the method will realize the difficulty of the problem. Theoretically, maximum likelihood estimation should give better results, but it is still harder to apply.

Day (1969) used the maximum likelihood approach to estimate the components of mixtures of both univariate and multivariate normal distributions. He showed that the use of electronic computers made a solution possible in practice, at least for the case of equal dispersion matrices, and discussed the difficulties that can make the situation intractable.

The maximum likelihood method is primarily adapted for large sample investigations, and this is very much the case here. Each p-variate normal distribution involves $\frac{1}{2}p$ $(p + 3)$ parameters, and they can only be estimated if each distribution is represented by a large sample. There is a real risk that, even when the groups seem well separated, the problem is over-parameterized, and estimation becomes impossible. When the grouping is doubtful, or samples are inadequate, the estimates may become quite unrealistic.

Further constraints make the difficulties less severe, but also make the approach less general. For example, estimation becomes much simpler if the dispersion matrix is assumed to be the same in all groups. This assumption is often unrealistic, and the weaker assumption of the same *correlation* matrix may be sufficient to make the method practicable.

As a technique for cluster analysis, Day's method has the serious defect, from the practical point of view, that it assumes that the under-lying distributions are multivariate normal. Mixtures of normal distributions may have almost any shape, and most experimental scientists would not be prepared to say that a skew distribution, or one with positive or negative kurtosis, was necessarily a mixture of two or more normal distributions. This is equally true in the multivariate case; it is usually unrealistic to assume that each variate is normally distributed, that they are related by simple correlations, and that any departure from this situation is a result of mixing.

Day's method is almost the only classification technique that is entirely satisfactory from the mathematical point of view. It assumes a well defined mathematical model, investigates it by well established statistical techniques, and provides a test of significance for the results. The fact that it is difficult to apply, and in many situations unrealistic, reflects the complexity of the question that cluster analysis is trying to answer. Other methods avoid many of the difficulties of Day's method, apparently make fewer assumptions, and seem to work quite well in certain situations, but their mathematical basis is less secure, and it is nearly always possible to find situations in which they give misleading answers.

In summary, Day's technique—regarded as a method of cluster analysis, rather than as a pure estimation problem—has the advantages:

(i) it is mathematically sound;

(ii) it adopts a well defined model, and provides estimates and tests of significance.

Its disadvantages are practical:

(i) it assumes underlying normal distributions in a situation where the central limit theorem gives no protection;

(ii) it implies that a large sample is available from each group;
(iii) the numerical analysis is difficult.

4. Wishart's method: direct search for modes

Wishart (1968) proposed an entirely different approach to numerical classification. If the criterion for the separation of groups is to be that of multimodality, an obvious line of attack is to look for modes. Wishart did this by defining "dense points" as the centres of hyperspheres of minimum radius containing a given number of points, and then expanding the hyperspheres to associate the other points with them. During this expansion there is a continuous revision, the dense points moving to give minimum radius to the sphere associated with the number of points contained, and new dense points being defined as the radius increases.

The process continues until all points have been classified, and at this stage they are divided into a number of groups giving the final classification. During the expansion, new group centres may emerge, and groups already formed may be combined. The final number of groups may be one only, if the distribution has not more than one well marked mode.

The process depends on one parameter: the number of points defining the original dense points. It is an agglomerative hierarchical procedure, and if this parameter $k = 1$, it reduces to ordinary single-link clustering. Nevertheless, when $k > 1$ it differs from other hierarchical techniques in its aims and conclusions. The purpose of the analysis is to find a natural grouping, and the intermediate steps are of no importance. It is theoretically possible to construct a dendrogram to represent the steps leading to the final grouping, but the intermediate stages consist of one or more groups and a number of isolated points.

The method is suitable for clustering either continuous variates or binary variates. It is not satisfactory for a mixture of the two, and discrete or coarsely grouped variates are apt to be troublesome. The definition of dense points avoids any assumption of an underlying distribution, and there is no sampling theory or significance test associated with the method. The aim is to detect clustering of the observations. If, in fact, the data are a sample from a distribution of some sort, it is not clear how effective the method is at rejecting spurious clustering due to sampling fluctuations; this depends on the value chosen for k. At least, if k is not very small, it will not suggest a grouping when the data give no indication of heterogeneity.

One defect of the method is that the definition of dense points in

terms of spheres makes it less effective when variates are highly correlated and the contours surrounding the modes are elongated ellipses.
The difficulty could be overcome in the case of continuous variables by
working with principal coordinates scaled to the same variance, but
Wishart does not recommend this.

Though it is technically a variation of agglomerative hierarchical
clustering, the possibility of varying k gives Wishart's method far
greater flexibility than other methods in this class. If the aim is to find
a natural grouping, rather than to construct a dendrogram, it is
effective and unlikely to give misleading results. On the whole, it is
probably the best practical classification technique at present available.

In summary, Wishart's method has the following advantages:

(i) it is a direct approach designed to identify the modes of the
underlying distribution, or the clustering of the results;

(ii) it is unlikely to suggest a completely spurious grouping;

(iii) no sampling theory is invoked—though when the observations
really are a sample, the properties of the method are not known.

Its weaknesses are:

(i) it is suitable only for either continuous observations or binary
observations;

(ii) for continuous variates, rather large samples may be needed;

(iii) it is insensitive in detecting elongated modes;

(iv) the choice of the value of k may affect the conclusions.

5. Minimizing Wilks' criterion (Friedman and Rubin)

Friedman and Rubin (1967) discussed divisive methods of classification based on optimizing some statistic dependent on the grouping.
The principle is to find the best division into g groups, for $g = 2, 3, 4 \ldots$,
and then choose the best value of g. The method is not hierarchical; the
divisions for different values of g are made quite independently, and
each is the best possible for that particular value, according to the
criterion adopted.

The most interesting of these methods was based on minimizing the
generalized variance $|\mathbf{W}|$ within the groups. This is an extremely
plausible approach; the test of significance for differences between
groups in the generalized analysis of variance is based on Wilks'
criterion (see Chapter 3) and a grouping that minimizes this statistic
(or equivalently minimizes the generalized variance) is, in some sense,
an optimum grouping.

There is, however, one serious theoretical flaw in this reasoning. If
the data consist of samples from a mixture of unimodal distributions,
the groups defined by this procedure will be the truncated centres of

these distributions, mixed with the tails of other distributions. The dispersion matrix estimated within groups will not be an estimate of the dispersion matrix of the underlying distributions, even if these are identical, and there is no reason to expect that it will be the same within the artificial groups found by the clustering process.

Scott and Symons (1971) showed that the application of maximum likelihood methods to the problem of identifying mixtures of multivariate normal distributions with unknown, but identical, dispersion matrices led to clustering by minimizing Wilks' criterion. Their approach was to estimate, by maximum likelihood, the p means, the $\frac{1}{2}p$ $(p-1)$ variances and covariances, and N identifying parameters that assign the N sample points to the postulated g groups.

The resulting estimates indicated that the identifying parameters should be chosen to minimize $|\mathbf{W}|$, and the maximum likelihood estimates of the means and variances and covariances were then given by the means of groups formed, and the sample variances and covariances within groups, in the usual way.

The conclusion, however, is misleading. Clearly the latter estimates are not consistent; if there is considerable overlap, the means of the groups may be far from the means of the underlying normal distributions. In fact, maximum likelihood estimators do not have their usual desirable properties when the number of parameters to be estimated increases indefinitely with the sample size—this point has already been noted in connexion with factor analysis (see Chapter 6, Section B). The justification of Friedman and Rubin's method as maximum likelihood applied to a mixture of normal distributions is therefore not altogether successful, although it leads to a reasonable allocation rule.

Marriott (1971) tried to circumvent this difficulty by assuming a uniform distribution as a null hypothesis. It is possible to predict the effect of an optimum subdivision on the generalized variance $|\mathbf{W}|$ if the null hypothesis is true, and if the subdivision of the data reduces the generalized variance by much more than this, for any value of g, it is reasonable to suppose that it corresponds to a natural grouping of the data.

In fact, this suggestion works reasonably well. An optimum subdivision of a uniform distribution into g groups reduces $|\mathbf{W}|$ by a factor g^2. A strongly multimodal distribution will be reduced much more than this when it is appropriately divided, while most ordinary unimodal distributions will be reduced less. The criterion is not equivalent to that of multimodality. When the modes are near together and the distributions overlap considerably, separation may be impossible even for very large samples. On the other hand, some peculiar unimodal distributions of an extremely leptokurtic type may be sub-divided. Nevertheless, the criterion for subdivision accords reasonably well with a subjective judgment of what sort of distribution should be regarded as composite.

The problems of numerical analysis, as with all divisive methods, are formidable. Rubin (1967) has devised a procedure which he claims will nearly always reach the unique optimum grouping. This is based on successive improvement of an assumed subdivision, but incorporates, as well as transfers of single items, more substantial rearrangements of the data.

The sampling theory, on the basis of the null hypothesis, is also difficult. When g varies, the value of $g^2 \mid \mathbf{W} \mid$ should remain approximately constant for large samples. In practice, it will tend to decrease as g increases, because the best subdivision for the particular sample being considered will give a lower value than the theoretical optimum division for the population. A full theoretical investigation of the sampling distribution would be valuable. As it has not been done, the best approach to the problem seems to be to plot $g^2 \mid \mathbf{W} \mid$ against g; if the graph decreases steadily, there is no indication of a natural grouping, but if for one value of g the value of $g^2 \mid \mathbf{W} \mid$ falls well below the neighbouring values, it suggests that this corresponds to a natural grouping.

The following points were made by Marriott (1971):

(i) Heterogeneity of the dispersion matrices of the components can result in excessive subdivision. This can be remedied by recombining any two sections that *by themselves* would not suggest that separation was necessary.

(ii) Different proportions in the components may displace the divisions between them. There is a tendency to overestimate the space, and the proportion, allotted to a smaller group, but the effect is probably not seriously misleading.

(iii) The method is intended for continuous variates. Grouped data or discrete variates can be included, but only with the use of a grouping correction added to the sample variance.

(iv) Concomitant observations can be incorporated quite easily. It is only necessary to minimize a modified determinant.

In summary, the advantages of this method are:

(i) great flexibility, in the data that can be handled and in the use of concomitant observations;

(ii) independence of scale and of linear transformations.

Its disadvantages are:

(i) the mathematical basis is not altogether solid; in particular, the criterion for subdivision is rather arbitrary;

(ii) a significance test, though theoretically possible, does not yet exist;

(iii) the computations are heavy.

6. Hybrid methods

Apart from the formal techniques of cluster analysis already discussed, the structure of multivariate data may be studied by methods that combine different approaches. Once a provisional grouping has been formed, it can be used to calculate discriminant functions, which can then be used to modify the grouping. Alternatively, canonical variables based on the provisional grouping can be used for ordination, and if the grouping is a reasonable one, may be more informative than principal components used in the same way.

The main advantage of this sort of approach is that subsidiary information, perhaps derived from previous studies, or on impressions that are difficult to quantify, can be incorporated into the original grouping. This need not apply to all the observations; the provisional groups may consist of items regarded as typical of the groups in a subjective classification, and the further analysis will then assign the remaining observations to the appropriate classes, or perhaps to new classes, as the results seem to suggest.

This sort of heuristic approach obviously involves a considerable subjective element, and accordingly requires skill and knowledge if it is to be used effectively. If other methods of cluster analysis were completely satisfactory in all situations, these hybrid methods might become obsolete; as it is, they have proved valuable. Du Praw (1965) has used techniques of this type in numerical taxonomy, and Webster and Burroughs (1973) in soil science.

7. Problems of binary variables

The problem of classification when all the variates recorded are binary is an important one, with many applications. In particular, numerical taxonomy is usually concerned with data of this type. Probably more published papers on cluster analysis deal with binary data than with any other situation.

If p binary variates are recorded, the data can be expressed in the form of a 2^p contingency table. Now, it is intuitively clear that if the variates are completely independent, as indicated, for example, by a χ^2 test, there can be no justification for postulating any sort of grouping. The existence of an underlying natural grouping must reveal itself, if at all, in the dependencies between the variates. Certainly there can be no question of eliminating such dependencies before looking for evidence of clustering.

A corollary of this point is that any variables that are non-independent for reasons not connected with an underlying grouping should not be included in the analysis. For example, variables associated with the size of the organism, or variables that reflect adaptation to a particular environment, will tend to suggest groupings based on these features, and often this is not the sort of grouping that the taxonomist is looking for. The selection of variables for analysis, important in any multivariate procedure, is paramount in the case of binary variables.

Given a set of binary variables, the problem of deciding whether there is more than one group, and if so how many, and how they should be divided, is not an easy one. Often there will be clustering about two or more vertices of the imaginary hypercube defined by the variables, and so an intuitive basis for subdivision. This is the idea behind Wishart's method of cluster analysis; but the justification for multimodality as a criterion is less clear in the case of binary variates than in that of continuous variates. Consider, for example, the simplest case of a double dichotomy represented by a fourfold table. If both characters divide the data into equal proportions, non-independence implies bimodality. If, on the other hand, the proportions are very different from $\frac{1}{2}$, much stronger dependence is needed before the highest frequencies appear in the diagonal cells. On the other hand, if the dichotomies correspond to a dissection of an underlying continuous distribution, there is no simple connexion between the number of modes of this distribution and of the derived distribution of the binary variates. In general, multimodality depends in a complicated way on the probabilities associated with each dichotomy and the dependencies among them.

Lazarsfeld and Henry (1968) have suggested basing clustering (and other multivariate techniques) on a direct consideration of the dependencies among the variates. They have developed a battery of methods, under the general description of Latent Structure Analysis, on a postulate they name the Axiom of Local Independence. This states: "Within a latent class, α, responses to different items are independent. The within class probability of any pattern of response to any set of items is the product of the appropriate marginal probabilities."

The consequences of this axiom are worked out in detail, and give rise to the probabilities for each possible combination of characters for each of the postulated underlying groups. These probabilities can be used to assign different combinations to the appropriate group, and to estimate misclassification probabilities. The mathematical difficulties are considerable, and so are the problems of computation, but provided the axiom is satisfied, a solution with the right number of groups can be found.

These latent structure models were developed in the field of the social sciences, and most of the illustrative examples are taken from this discipline. The method, nevertheless, is perfectly general. It is a complete solution to the problem of cluster analysis for binary variates in cases where the axiom of local independence is an acceptable criterion of clustering.

In fact, the whole approach stands or falls by the validity of the axiom. It states that *all* relationships between the characters must be accountable for by the underlying group structure. If the experimenter is satisfied that this is true, there is no doubt that latent structure analysis is the appropriate technique for estimating the parameters of the structure. In many practical situations, however, the axiom does not seem to be satisfied. Examination of the data suggests a fairly clear division into groups, but within these groups there are still dependencies among the variates. In these circumstances, estimation of parameters by a latent structure analysis may give quite unacceptable values. This is not surprising; the method depends on a strictly defined model, and if the model does not fit the data the estimation procedures naturally break down.

It is clear that latent structure analysis is not the complete answer to the problem of cluster analysis for binary data. In many practical situations, the structure imposed by the axiom of local independence is too rigid. Particularly when the number of variates is large, the model may not fit the data even when there is clear evidence of what seems intuitively to be a natural grouping. This perhaps accounts for the lack of applications in the biological sciences.

In conclusion, the method of latent structure analysis has the advantages:

(i) it offers a clearly defined model that gives unique and unambiguous answers to the problem of cluster analysis where it is appropriate;

(ii) it is mathematically and logically sound.

The disadvantages are:

(i) The assumptions are rigid, and unrealistic in many practical situations;

(ii) it presents difficult mathematical and computational problems.

Since the main drawback of the method lies in the strictness of the axiom of local independence, it seems worth considering whether the axiom might be modified to give a criterion for clustering that would be more widely applicable while preserving the simplicity and clarity of the original assumption. One might, for example, allow non-independence within groups while excluding higher order interactions in the sense of Bartlett (1935). Alternatively, one might postulate a multivariate logistic distribution (Cox, 1972) with parameters determined by group membership. Anderson's (1974) approach to factor analysis for binary variates is an indication of how this criterion might be formulated. Unfortunately, the mathematical difficulties are formidable, and so far no practical technique is available.

8. Conclusions

The foregoing summary of a few of the more popular methods of cluster analysis illustrates the complexity of the problem and the number of possible approaches. To some extent it reflects the variety of problems that seem to require some form of cluster analysis, but it is also an indication of confusion about aims and about the properties of different methods. As things stand at present, I believe that Wishart's method is the best available for detecting and identifying a natural grouping. It is unlikely to produce a meaningless or misleading answer, a well-tested program exists, and it is applicable to most practical situations.

I suggest further that the results of any cluster analysis, whatever method has been used, should be accompanied by scatter diagrams, based on principal components or canonical variates, to illustrate how the clusters found relate to the distribution of the points. A reader sceptical about the numerical analysis (as he well might be) can then judge for himself how well the proposed clusters reflect the structure of the data.

9
Examples

A. THE EGYPTIAN SKULLS

A much-analysed example of classical discriminant analysis is provided by the series of Egyptian skulls measured by Barnard (1935). These comprised 398 specimens, divided into four groups dating from different periods, as follows:

I. Predynastic ($n_1 = 91$).
II. Dynasties 6 to 12 ($n_2 = 162$).
III. Dynasties 12 and 13 ($n_3 = 70$).
IV. Ptolemaic dynasties ($n_4 = 75$).

Four measurements were taken on each skull, as follows:

x_1 Maximum breadth.
x_2 Basi-alveolar length.
x_3 Nasal height.
x_4 Basi-bregmatic height.

The data are unusual in that they conform reasonably well with all the assumptions of classical multivariate statistics. The measurements are of a type that is known to be at least approximately normally distributed; there is reason to expect that changes in the mean values from period to period will be more important than changes in variability or in the correlations between measurements; and in the data as presented there are no complications with doubtful assignments or missing values. It is known that the time intervals between the series are roughly in the ratio $2:1:2$, and the problem is to interpret the differences between the measurements in the four groups.

The first step is to examine the means (Table 9.I). It is clear that x_1 shows a steady increase, and x_2 a steady decrease, through the four periods. Further, the changes in both variables are, at least roughly, in line with the known time scale; the differences between series II and III are less than those between I and II, and between III and IV. On the other hand, x_3 and x_4 show irregular variations that, if they are not merely random fluctuations, suggest that the changes observed cannot be interpreted as regular temporal development.

Tables 9.II and 9.III show the matrices of sums of squares and products within groups and about the overall means respectively. It is easy to check that analyses of variance on each of the four variables show highly significant differences between the groups. There are positive correlations within groups between each pair of variables, but none of these is very large. It therefore seems likely that, while the first two measurements may reflect steady temporal changes, the other two show that such variation cannot account for all the observed differences.

Wilks' criterion, $L = |\mathbf{W}| / |\mathbf{T}| = 0 \cdot 82$, and the corresponding χ^2 with 12 d.f. is $77 \cdot 3$. This is obviously highly significant. The individual canonical correlations are given by $1_1{}^2 = 0 \cdot 1098$, $1_2{}^2 = 0 \cdot 0596$, $1_3{}^2 = 0 \cdot 0187$. The first is obviously highly significant; the exact significance probability (Marriott, 1952) is $3 \cdot 1 \times 10^{-7}$. Assuming that this corresponds to a genuine relationship, the second canonical correlation can be tested with $p = 2$, $q = 3$. The exact probability (Marriott, 1952) is $1 \cdot 7 \times 10^{-4}$. The approximate χ^2 test gives a value $24 \cdot 17$, with $4 + \frac{1}{2} . 2^{2/3} = 4 \cdot 8$. d.f. The corresponding probability agrees well (Pearson and Hartley, 1972, give a table of percentage points of χ^2 with non-integral d.f.) Finally, assuming that the first two canonical correlations represent real differences, the third can be tested by an exact F test, since the case $p = 1$, $q = 2$ is equivalent to a simple multiple regression. This gives $F = 3 \cdot 68$, $P = 0 \cdot 025$.

Since the second (and the third) canonical correlation is significant, it is clear that the variation in the measurements cannot be purely due to temporal variation, of any form, in a linear function of the measurements. Table 9.IV shows the three canonical variables as functions of the measurements, and the mean values for the four groups. Interpretation is easy, though not very interesting. The first canonical variable separates group IV from the rest, the second similarly isolates group I, and the third distinguishes group III from the others.

The pattern of the differences among the groups can be confirmed by calculating the generalized distances between each pair. Table 9.V shows the values of D. It is easy to construct a tetrahedron with edges equal to the values of D, and to compare the shape of the tetrahedron with the canonical variables. There is good agreement between the two; in general, such agreement will not necessarily be so close, since the distances do not depend directly on the numbers in the groups, but here the numbers are not too different, and the distances clearly show the same distinctions as the canonical variables.

Table 9.V also gives the F values for testing each distance. These have 4 and 391 d.f., and each is very nearly $D^2/4(1/n_i + 1/n_j)$. It is

TABLE 9.I

Mean values of skull measurements (Barnard, 1935)

	Series I	Series II	Series III	Series IV
x_1	133·58	134·27	134·37	135·31
x_2	98·31	96·46	95·86	95·04
x_3	50·84	51·15	50·10	52·09
x_4	133·00	134·88	133·64	131·47
	$n_1 = 91$	$n_2 = 162$	$n_3 = 70$	$n_4 = 75$

TABLE 9.II

S.O.S. and S.O.P. matrix within groups

	x_1	x_2	x_3	x_4
x_1	9662·00	445·57	1130·62	2148·58
x_2		9073·12	1239·22	2255·81
x_3			3938·32	1271·05
x_4				8741·51

TABLE 9.III

S.O.S. and S.O.P. matrix (total)

	x_1	x_2	x_3	x_4
x_1	9785·18	214·20	1217·93	2019·82
x_2		9559·46	1131·72	2381·13
x_3			4088·73	1133·47
x_4				9382·24

The values in Tables 9.I–9.III are rounded off from the original published values (Bartlett, 1947b).

TABLE 9.IV

Coefficients and mean values of the canonical variables (not adjusted to zero mean)

First canonical variable.			
$y_1 = -0.071x_1 + 0.070x_2 - 0.190x_3 + 0.167x_4$			
Series I	II	III	IV
9·96	10·04	9·98	9·11

Second canonical variable.			
$y_2 = 0.024x_1 - 0.187x_2 + 0.043x_3 + 0.142x_4$			
Series I	II	III	IV
5·80	6·44	6·33	6·29

Third canonical variable.			
$y_3 = -0.064x_1 + 0.046x_2 + 0.266x_3 + 0.060x_4$			
Series I	II	III	IV
17·56	17·62	17·23	17·53

TABLE 9.V

Values of D, with corresponding F values in parentheses

Series	I	II	III	IV
I		0·65 (6·14)	0·63 (3·87)	0·98 (9·82)
II			0·41 (2·02)	0·94 (7·64)
III				0·92 (7·64)

interesting that the distance between groups II and III does not reach significance, in apparent contradiction with the finding that the third canonical correlation is significant. The distinction between the two tests is that the test of generalized distance applies to an arbitrary comparison between two groups, while that for the third canonical correlation takes account of the fact that the corresponding variable is orthogonal to the first and second canonical variables, which have been selected to account for as much as possible of the variability among the groups. Although the two tests refer, practically speaking, to the same variable, the canonical correlation test takes account of the fact that the variable is selected after other comparisons have been made.

B. LOCOMOTOR DISCRIMINATION IN PRIMATES

An outstanding example of the use of numerical methods in a taxonomic study is given by the work of Ashton *et al.* (1965) on the primate shoulder girdle. A set of nine variates was used for the study, consisting of angles and indices based on measurements of the scapula. The variates, all being ratios, did not directly relate to the size of the animals. The material consisted of 458 individuals, divided into 34 races; the "races" were genera with two minor exceptions, baboons and mandrills being considered together, and *Presbytis* being subdivided into three groups according to habitat.

The first step was to carry out a canonical analysis. It was found that the first three canonical variates gave significant discrimination among the races. In considering the grouping of the races, therefore, only these three variates needed to be studied instead of the original nine, a valuable reduction in dimensionality.

The true apes were divided into three groups according to their method of locomotion. Four races—chimpanzees, gibbons, gorillas and orang-utans—were classed as brachiators, their main mode of progression being by swinging from branch to branch. Thirteen races were classed as quadrupeds, and the remaining ten as semi-brachiators. The Prosimii were divided into two groups: quadrupeds, including the lemur and bush-baby *Galago*, and the brachiating species or "hangers", including the potto and one of the loris group. The remaining genus was man.

The first canonical variate was easily identified as separating the groups according to this classification. The quadrupeds all had high values, showing no overlap with the other groups. The brachiators all had low values, and the semi-brachiators intermediate values, though here the separation was not perfect; the spider-monkeys *Ateles* and *Brachyteles*, classed as semi-brachiators, seemed on this criterion to belong rather to the brachiator group. The quadrupedal Prosimii fell among the quadrupeds, and the hangers among the semi-brachiators, and man was also in this intermediate group.

The meaning of the second canonical variate was less obvious. According to the authors, it gives some separation between the completely arboreal and the partially terrestrial types within the main locomotor groups, the former having low values of the variate and the latter high. Man, with the lowest value of all, is in an anomalous position, and on the basis of these two values might well be classified as an "outlier", clearly detached from the three main groups.

The third variate showed a much smaller range than the other two, apart from the extremely low value for man. In fact, this variate serves chiefly to separate man clearly from all the other races—within them, it seems to give no significant discrimination.

The values for the three variates are shown in Fig. 9.1. Each is standardized to have zero mean and unit variance within races, except that the values of variate 3 have been increased by 6 for ease of presentation. Groups A, B and C are the quadrupeds, semi-brachiators and brachiators as originally defined; *Ateles* and *Brachyteles* appear at the left hand end of the middle group. D is man, separated from the other groups by the low value of variate 2, and still more by the extremely low value of variate 3. Groups E and F are the

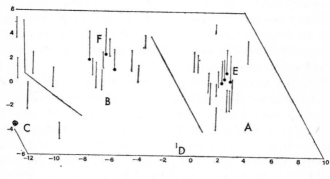

FIG. 9.1

A plot of the first three canonical variates for the data on the primate shoulder-girdle. The first variable, shown as the abscissa, is closely related to the mode of locomotion. The second has some relationship to arboreal or terrestrial habitat within the groups indicated by the first, and separates man from the main group of semi-brachiators; it is shown as the ordinate. The third is shown by the length of the lines, which is proportional to the value of the variate +6. It clearly separates man from the other primates, but otherwise gives little discrimination between races.

The letters show the races classified by their means of locomotion, independently of the canonical analysis. The Prosimii are distinguished by dots. Group A are the quadrupeds, group E being the quadrupedal Prosimii, in no way differentiated from the anthropoidal quadrupeds by the canonical analysis. Group B are the semi-brachiators, and group F the "hangers" among the Prosimii. Group C are the brachiators; the two races at the extreme left of group B are *Ateles* and *Brachyteles*, which the numerical analysis would class as brachiators rather than semi-brachiators. The point D is man, separated from the other primates by the low values of variates 2 and 3.

quadrupeds and hangers among the Prosimii; there is no suggestion that they can be separated from the true apes on the basis of these measurements of the scapula. They form fairly compact groups within these larger groups. (One item in Group E is *Daubentonia*, the aye-aye, a quadrupedal prosimian not included among the original 34 groups, but with variate values computed later from a single specimen.)

This study is a very successful example of a hybrid method of cluster analysis. The use of canonical variates was possible because several members of each group were available for study. Probably principal components would give very similar results, but canonical variates have the great advantage that those that show no significant discrimination between races can be left out of consideration in grouping the races. With principal components there is no objective criterion for deciding how many variates should be considered.

The classification achieved is quite distinct from the conventional taxonomy of the races. Apart from the failure to discriminate between the Prosimii and the Anthropoidea, certain recognized superfamilies have representatives in two of the groups. The clustering is on the basis of the way in which the shoulder is used, not on probable evolutionary relationships. It could be used to determine the likely mode of loco-motion of an extinct species, rather than its position in the conventional taxonomy of the primates.

C. STUDIES OF SOIL CLASSIFICATION AND MAPPING

Webster (1972) and Webster and Burrough (1973) studied different methods of classifying soils and making general-purpose soil maps. A general-purpose classification of soils is an attempt to group soils in such a way that the users of the resulting map, whether their interest is in agriculture, building or mining, may find it informative. In other words, the soils are to be grouped into units that are as homogeneous as possible, not with respect to a single character, but to a whole range. The characters are selected as being either themselves important to some of the potential users, or indicative of characteristics of the soil that are of interest.

The problem is essentially one of dissection; the classes may be "natural" groups, representing distinct soil types that seldom occur in mixtures or intermediate forms, or they may be merely a convenient subdivision of a continuous range. Whether natural classes exist depends on the choice of characters, the population sampled, and the criterion adopted for a natural class. If they do, they will probably give a convenient dissection, possibly with some modification in the way of combining very small groups or subdividing very large ones.

Webster and Burrough studied three areas in the Oxford district, each 600 m × 1400 m, on very different soil types. Each was sampled at the intersections of a 100 m grid, giving 84 sample points. At each of these sites, about 30 properties were recorded. Not all of these were used in the subsequent analysis; for example, in one area properties were taken from the first two horizons, namely the plough layer, about 20 cm deep, and the layer immediately below it. The properties used for analysis were, in the area discussed here:

in each horizon, Munsell hue, value and chroma, $CaCO_3$, and clay (but in this area the hue of the first horizon was invariant and therefore omitted from the analysis);

in the first horizon, in addition, organic matter, cation exchange capacity, pH, exchangeable Mg and K, and available P;

depth to $CaCO_3$, and total penetrable depth.

There were thus 17 properties, which were treated as separate variates on the same footing. In this case, when one is dealing with two distinct horizons of which the first was of more or less constant depth, the procedure is reasonable.

The soils were classified by an experienced soil surveyor (M. G. Jarvis) into two, three, and four groups. "At the 2-class level they were divided into brown earth and rendzina. At the 3-class level the brown earth group was split into two series, Charity and Coombe, while the rendzina was considered to be a single series, Icknield. At the 4-class level Icknield was split into grey and brown variants, while Charity and Coombe remained undivided." It is notable that the soil surveyor adopted a strictly hierarchical strategy; at each stage groups were subdivided, or combined, without transferring any sites from one group to another.

A separate numerical classification was carried out by the strictly hierarchical method of Sokal and Sneath (1963). Three different dissimilarity measures were tried; simple Euclidean distance, Euclidean distance after standardization, and the "Canberra metric", defined by

$$D_{ij} = \frac{1}{p} \sum_{k=1}^{p} |X_{ik} - X_{jk}| / (X_{ik} + X_{jk})$$

The first of these measures proved least satisfactory; the other two gave very similar results. In the later study, the Canberra metric was used, and the discussion here will be confined to that.

The success of the classification was judged using Wilks' criterion, in the way suggested by Marriott (1971). Both the systematic classification by the soil surveyor and the numerical classification showed a minimum value of g^2L at $g = 3$. This suggests that there is indeed a "natural" subdivision into three soil types, as suggested by the surveyor's conclusions. The most notable feature, however, was the great superiority, judged by a purely numerical criterion, of the surveyor's subjective assessment to the classification produced by a standard technique of cluster analysis.

In view of the criticisms of hierarchical techniques in the last chapter, it would be tempting to attribute the failure to this feature of the analysis. Of course the Friedman-Rubin clustering procedure based on minimizing L would have produced results at least as good, judged by that criterion, as the subjective classification. Nevertheless, since the surveyor himself adopted a hierarchical strategy, this cannot be the explanation. In fact, it seems clear that there are three distinct soil classes present, and the numerical technique has failed to find them.

Webster and Burrough (1973) examined the numerical and systematic classifications in more detail. The first subdivision by the numerical method corresponded roughly to the surveyor's brown earth and rendzina categories. (The algorithm was, in fact, agglomerative, but it is easier to discuss the reverse process.) The second subdivision divided the "brown earth" group, but the split did not correspond to the surveyor's classes, Coombe and Charity. Interestingly, the numerically determined classes were geographically more compact, although the program took no account of position. The subdivisions into four and five classes split off into separate groups respectively two and one sites, with, correspondingly, rather small reductions in the value of L. The six and seven class partitionings produced rather larger new classes, with larger reductions in L, but only the 7-class split brought the value below that corresponding to the surveyor's three soil series.

Webster and Burrough went on to discuss ordination of the soils using principal components based on the correlation matrix. The first principal component accounted for 40.4% of the total variance. It seemed to be quite strongly associated with the drainage properties of the soil. A histogram showing the frequency distribution of this component showed three distinct modes, and these corresponded reasonably well to the soil series, Icknield, Coombe and Charity (Figs. 9.2, 9.3). The second principal component accounted for a further 14.5% of the total variance. It was less easy to interpret, but since organic matter in the first horizon, cation exchange capacity, and Mg all featured strongly, it was probably considerably dependent on differences in management. It was unrelated to the surveyor's classification—not surprisingly, since soil surveyors generally try to disregard the effects of management.

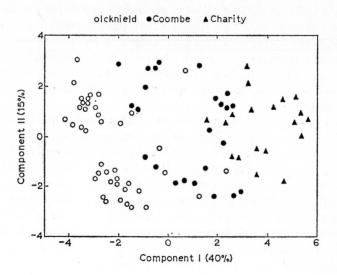

FIG. 9.2

Scatter diagram showing the distribution of the first two principal components for the soils at 84 sites. The soil surveyor's classification is shown by different symbols. They correspond reasonably well to the values of the first component, which reflected primarily differences in drainage. The second component also seems to indicate some grouping, but one quite unrelated to the surveyor's classification. The measurements featuring most prominently in this component related to the chemical composition of the topsoil, and probably reflected differences in management more than in soil type.

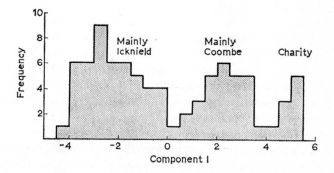

FIG. 9.3

Histogram of the first principal component of the data in Fig. 9.2. The histogram shows clear evidence of three modes. The three groups correspond closely, but not exactly, to the surveyor's classification.

The last part of the paper discussed the problem of smoothing the soil classification. Clearly in preparing a soil map it is undesirable to have excessive geographical fragmentation; to some extent, the class assigned to a site should depend on that of the nearby sites, to avoid the appearance of too many isolated patches on the map. This is a specialized problem outside the scope of this book, but it is interesting that the most effective method tried involved weighting the dissimilarity, or distance in character space, by a function increasing with the geographical distance. This is an example of the flexibility of methods based on dissimilarity.

These papers are an interesting and valuable contribution to the practice of multivariate methods because they apply a number of different techniques to the same, fairly small, body of data. It seems clear that the problem of classifying the soils involved was solved successfully by the soil surveyor, and by the simple ordination procedure using principal components. On the other hand, hierarchical numerical classification produced quite different, and clearly inferior, results. This emphasizes, once again, the importance of examining critically the results of any form of cluster analysis. If the results disagree with informed opinion, do not admit a simple logical interpretation, and do not show up clearly in a graphical presentation, they are probably wrong. There is no magic about numerical methods, and many ways in which they can break down. They are a valuable aid to the interpretation of data, not sausage machines automatically transforming bodies of numbers into packets of scientific fact.

Elements of Matrix Algebra

A. INTRODUCTION

A great deal of the mathematics in statistical calculations is concerned with two very elementary ideas, maximizing and minimizing quadratic forms, and solving the resulting linear equations. These problems occur so often that it is useful to adopt an abbreviated notation and some special conventions for dealing with them. This is what matrix algebra is about. The fundamental ideas are very simple, and essentially matrix algebra is a formalized, abbreviated, notation for handling large numbers of simultaneous equations. It is valuable because it is widely used in, for example, the specification of computer programs and in statistical papers, and because it saves a lot of writing.

Suppose a set of simultaneous linear equations express the m variables $y_1 \ldots y_m$ in terms of the n variables $x_1 \ldots x_n$. The equations may be written:

$$y_1 = a_{11}x_1 + a_{12}x_2 \ldots + a_{1n}x_n$$
$$y_2 = a_{21}x_1 + a_{22}x_2 \ldots + a_{2n}x_n$$
$$\ldots$$
$$y_m = a_{1m}x_1 + a_{m2}x_2 \ldots + a_{mn}x_n$$

In these equations, one convention has already been adopted; a_{ij} is the coefficient of the jth variable in the ith equation—and not the other way round.

Another way of writing these equations is to separate the coefficients from the variables, and write them in the form:

$$\begin{pmatrix} y_1 \\ y_2 \\ \vdots \\ y_m \end{pmatrix} = \begin{pmatrix} a_{11}\, a_{12} \ldots a_{1n} \\ a_{21}\, a_{22} \ldots a_{2n} \\ \ldots \\ a_{m1}\, a_{m2} \ldots a_{mn} \end{pmatrix} \begin{pmatrix} x_1 \\ x_2 \\ \vdots \\ x_n \end{pmatrix}$$

In this way of writing the equations, the columns of variables are called *vectors*, and the array of coefficients is called an $m \times n$ *matrix*. Notice that m refers to the number of rows, and the second suffix n to the number of columns. When the equations are written out in full, the elements of the rows of the matrix are the coefficients of the column on the left.

This set of equations is now abbreviated by writing

$$\mathbf{y} = \mathbf{Ax}$$

where **x** and **y** stand for the column vectors, and **A** represents the array of coefficients. Thus the set of equations is expressed as a shortened form, analogous to the simple equation $y = ax$.

It is sometimes useful to write $\mathbf{A} = (a_{ij})$, giving the typical element, of the ith row and the jth column, to define the matrix **A**.

B. ELEMENTARY MATRIX MANIPULATIONS

The addition and multiplication of the constants in simple equations suggests the possibility of doing the same sort of thing with matrices. For example, if $\mathbf{y} = \mathbf{Ax}$ and $\mathbf{z} = \mathbf{Bx}$ are two sets of equations expressing the m variables y and the m variables z in terms of the n variables x, it is easy to express the m variables $py + qz$ in terms of the x's. It is natural to write $py + qz = (p\mathbf{A} + q\mathbf{B})\mathbf{x}$, and it is easy to see that these equations are true if the matrix $p\mathbf{A} + q\mathbf{B}$ has as its i,jth element $pa_{ij} + qb_{ij}$. In other words, if **A** and **B** are $m \times n$ matrices and p and q are constants, the matrix $p\mathbf{A} + q\mathbf{B}$ is defined to have elements given by adding p times the elements of **A** and q times the corresponding elements of **B**. In particular, the matrix $\mathbf{A} + \mathbf{B}$ is formed by adding the corresponding elements of the two matrices. It is important to notice that these matrices are defined only when **A** and **B** have the same number of rows and columns.

In the same way, if $\mathbf{y} = \mathbf{Ax}$ and $\mathbf{z} = \mathbf{By}$, it is natural to write $\mathbf{z} = \mathbf{BAx}$. The first equation expresses the m variables y in terms of the x's by means of an $m \times n$ matrix. The second equation expresses the p variables z in terms of the y's by means of the matrix **B**, which must therefore have p rows and m columns. The matrix **BA** is *only* defined when the number of columns in **B** is equal to the number of rows in **A**. If **B** is $p \times m$ and **A** is $m \times n$, the product **BA** is a $p \times n$ matrix.

This brings out one of the most important differences between matrix algebra and ordinary algebra; multiplication is not commutative. The matrices **AB** and **BA** are not the same. They are both defined only if $m = n = p$, and even then they are, in general, different.

It is easy to verify, by substitution in the equations, that if $\mathbf{C} = \mathbf{BA}$,

$$c_{ij} = \sum_{k=1}^{m} b_{ik} a_{kj}.$$

Thus the product of two matrices is formed by multiplying the elements of the rows of the first by the corresponding elements of the columns of the second. The sum of products of the ith row of **B** with the jth column of **A** is the element of the ith row and jth column of **BA**.

If a matrix is formed from **A** by transposing the rows and columns, thus forming a $n \times m$ matrix with typical element a_{ji}, the resulting matrix is known as the *transpose* of **A**, and is written $\mathbf{A}'$. If $m = n$, **A** is said to be a *square* matrix. If **A** is a square matrix and $\mathbf{A} = \mathbf{A}'$, **A** is said to be a *symmetric* matrix.

If **A** and **B** are square $m \times m$ matrices and $\mathbf{C} = \mathbf{BA}$, then $\mathbf{C}' = \mathbf{A}'\mathbf{B}'$,

If $\mathbf{A}$ is symmetric, $\mathbf{B'AB}$ is also symmetric. The equation $\mathbf{y} = \mathbf{Ax}$ can also be written $\mathbf{y'} = \mathbf{x'A}$, where $\mathbf{y'}$ and $\mathbf{x'}$ are row vectors.

In many statistical applications, the matrices involved are symmetric. For example, all matrices of variances and covariances, of samples or populations, are symmetric. A correlation matrix is symmetric, with the elements a_{ii}, called the elements of the principal diagonal, equal to unity.

Finally, suppose $\mathbf{x}$ and $\mathbf{y}$ are column vectors with m elements, and $\mathbf{A}$ is a symmetric $m \times m$ matrix. Now $\mathbf{x'Ay}$ and $\mathbf{y'Ax}$ are called *bilinear forms*; it is easy to verify that they are the same single expression

$$\Sigma a_{ii} x_i y_i + 2 \sum_{i > j} a_{ij} x_i y_j.$$

The product reduces to a single element. When $\mathbf{x}$ and $\mathbf{y}$ are the same vector, the expression $\mathbf{x'Ax}$ is a *quadratic form* in the x's; any expression consisting of a sum of multiples of squares and products in pairs of the x's can be written in this form.

The *unit matrix* of order $m \times m$ is defined as the $m \times m$ matrix with unit elements in the leading diagonal and zeros elsewhere. It is denoted by $\mathbf{I}$. It is obvious that the equations $\mathbf{y} = \mathbf{x}$ and $\mathbf{y} = \mathbf{Ix}$ are the same.

If $\mathbf{A}$ is an $m \times m$ matrix, the equations $\mathbf{y} = \mathbf{Ax}$ can be solved to give the x's in terms of the y's, *provided* the m equations are not linearly dependent, that is, provided, it is not possible to write one of them as a linear combination of the others. It is then natural to write $\mathbf{x} = \mathbf{A^{-1}y}$, and $\mathbf{A^{-1}}$ is called the *inverse* of the matrix $\mathbf{A}$.

If the rows (or, equivalently, the columns) of $\mathbf{A}$ are linearly dependent, there are effectively fewer than m equations in the m unknowns, and there is no unique solution. In this case, $\mathbf{A}$ is said to be *singular*, and the inverse matrix is undefined. In the following sections, $\mathbf{A}$ will usually be assumed to be non-singular unless the point is discussed.

If $\mathbf{A^{-1}}$ exists, it is easy, in theory, to find it. The products $\mathbf{AA^{-1}}$ and $\mathbf{A^{-1}A}$ are both equal to the unit matrix $\mathbf{I}$. The matrix equation $\mathbf{AA^{-1}} = \mathbf{I}$ is equivalent to m sets of m simultaneous linear equations in the m^2 unknown elements of $\mathbf{A^{-1}}$, and the solution of each set of m equations gives the elements of one column of $\mathbf{A^{-1}}$. The problem of finding the inverse matrix is thus the problem of solving m sets of m simultaneous linear equations.

Although it is simple in theory, in practice the numerical calculations become very heavy when m is large. The inversion of matrices larger than about 5×5 is a tedious job when it has to be done on an electric calculating machine. Fortunately nowadays there are extremely efficient computer programs available, and inverse matrices with $m = 50$ or more can be computed without much trouble.

Thus all the elementary matrix manipulations have been defined. Division of matrices is not possible as such; since multiplication is not commutative, $\mathbf{A^{-1}B}$ and $\mathbf{BA^{-1}}$ are in general different, and the operation of division in ordinary algebra is replaced by either premultiplication or postmultiplication by the inverse matrix.

It is easy to verify that transposition and inversion of products of matrices reverse the order; thus $(\mathbf{AB})^{-1} = \mathbf{B}^{-1}\mathbf{A}^{-1}$, $(\mathbf{AB})' = \mathbf{B}'\mathbf{A}'$, $(\mathbf{ABC})^{-1} = \mathbf{C}^{-1}\mathbf{B}^{-1}\mathbf{A}^{-1}$, $(\mathbf{ABC})' = \mathbf{C}'\mathbf{B}'\mathbf{A}'$.

Apart from non-commutativity of multiplication, matrix manipulations obey all the rules of ordinary algebra. Thus quite complicated manipulations of sets of simultaneous equations can be written out algebraically with little more difficulty than simple algebraic equations. Numerical calculations are slow and tedious, and except for quite small matrices require the use of an electronic computer.

C. SINGULAR AND ILL-CONDITIONED MATRICES

This section is concerned with some of the numerical problems of matrix inversion. It does not involve any theory of matrix algebra.

In practical statistics, there is no reason to want the inverse of a singular matrix. For example, in multiple regression the problem of finding the best linear predictor becomes meaningless if the "independent" variables are in fact linearly related. Nevertheless, quite often a singular matrix is put into a computer program for inversion, usually as a result of a mistake.

Three common cases may be mentioned:

(i) One variable is, by definition, a linear combination of others; for example, total length may be the sum of head length, body length, and tail length. Clearly all four should not be included, but it is rather easy to do so when deciding which variables of a large group should be used for prediction.

(ii) One variable takes the same value for all items in a particular sample. Of course in that case it has no predictive value, but it may be included by mistake when many samples are analysed in a routine way.

(iii) When the sample size is small and data are grouped, the variables may be linearly related by chance. Of course, if the number of variables is as great as the sample size, there will always be a linear relationship.

What happens when a computer is asked to invert a singular matrix depends on the program.

In the first place, if no provision has been made for this contingency, the most likely result is an error signal "F. P. OVERFLOW". This means that at some point the computer has been asked to divide by zero. After tracing where the error occurred, the experimenter can work out that it must be because the matrix is singular, and can then change the data tape and start again.

It is a little more helpful if the computer gives a more specific error signal, such as "MATRIX COVAR IS SINGULAR". Still, however, the data tape must be altered, and there is no reason why the computer should not do the job itself.

In fact, if $\mathbf{y} = \mathbf{Ax}$ and $\mathbf{A}$ is a singular matrix, there is no difficulty in finding a matrix $\mathbf{B}$ such that $\mathbf{x} = \mathbf{By}$. The trouble is not that the equations are insoluble, but that they are indeterminate. There are infinitely many matrices $\mathbf{B}$ such that $\mathbf{AB} = \mathbf{I}$. They are known as generalized inverses of $\mathbf{A}$. One of them can be chosen by imposing additional conditions—the simplest and most useful is simply to omit one, or if necessary more, of the variables—and it gives a solution to the problem.

Accordingly, sophisticated computer programs, faced with the problem of inverting a singular matrix, use a generalized inverse and so give a solution, with an indication that this has been done and that the solution is not unique. It is then easy, if it is preferred, to transform the solution, for example to omit a different one of the dependent group of variables.

This is not the only application of generalized inverses; they can also be defined for matrices that are not square, and the theory of generalized inverses and their applications in numerical analysis has been very fully studied. For a detailed account, see Rao and Mitra (1971).

Another problem, in some ways more difficult, arises when matrices are *very nearly* singular. This can happen rather easily. For example, it may be perfectly reasonable to include log weight and log length in a regression equation, but for a group of organisms of very similar shape and density, they may be almost linearly related. A matrix which is almost singular, in the sense that a linear relationship between the variables applies except for very small variations of no physical importance, is called "ill-conditioned".

Manipulating ill-conditioned matrices involves difficulties of two sorts. In the first place, there are difficulties of numerical analysis; rounding-off errors in the calculations may become so important that a solution is found that is not even an acceptable approximation to the true solution. This is not a major problem in statistical work; if the matrix is as ill-conditioned as that, the exact numerical solution is unlikely to have any significance. The other difficulty is that the numerical solution may be meaningless. For example, if the regression of y on x_1 is $y = x_1$, and x_2 is very nearly equal to x_1, the regression of y on x_1 and x_2 may appear as $y = 1001x_1 - 998x_2$, the large coefficients being determined merely by tiny fluctuations in the measurements.

Of course, in the simple regression problem this situation is easy to recognize, because the standard errors of the coefficients would also be large, probably much larger than the coefficients themselves. No-one would then try to attach any physical meaning to the equation found. In more complicated situations, when standard errors are not known, there is a real possibility of trying to interpret a meaningless result.

There is no simple and reliable solution to this difficulty. It is important to be always aware of the possibility, and to consider whether there is a risk of very high correlations among the variables. Wherever possible, standard errors should be estimated, and the effect of leaving out some of the variables should be investigated. Otherwise, there is a danger of trying to reify expressions that have no real meaning, but are dependent on insignificant departures from a linear relationship.

D. DETERMINANTS

With any square matrix, there is associated a number called its *determinant*. For the $m \times m$ matrix **A** this number is derived from the $m!$ products that can be formed by m elements, one from each row and one from each column. There are $m!$ arrangements of the columns of **A**, and to each arrangement there corresponds a different principal diagonal. The $m!$ products are then the products of the terms of the principal diagonals in these arrangements. Each arrangement can be derived from the original matrix by interchanging a pair of columns, then another pair, and so on until the required arrangement is reached. If an *even* number of interchanges is required, the corresponding product has a *positive* sign, if an *odd* number of interchanges, the sign is *negative*. The determinant is the sum of these signed products.

Any particular arrangement can be derived in many different ways by interchanging products, and the number of interchanges is not fixed. It is easy to see, however, that the same arrangement cannot be derived both by an odd and an even number of interchanges, and this point is, of course, implicit in the definition of the determinant. In fact, $\frac{1}{2}(m!)$ terms have an associated positive sign, and $\frac{1}{2}(m!)$ a negative sign. Also, interchanging two columns (or two rows) of the matrix changes the sign of the determinant. This implies immediately that the determinant of a matrix with two identical columns or rows is zero.

As an example, if **A** is a 3×3 matrix, the determinant is:

$$a_{11}a_{22}a_{33} - a_{11}a_{23}a_{32} + a_{12}a_{23}a_{31} - a_{12}a_{21}a_{33} + a_{13}a_{22}a_{31} - a_{13}a_{22}a_{31}.$$

Of course, the sign attached to the terms in the product is not necessarily the sign of the numerical contributions; some of the terms in the original matrix may be negative. It is interesting, though, that if the matrix is symmetric there are always equal numbers of positive and negative numerical terms.

The most important property of the determinant is that it is zero if, and only if, the matrix is singular. If $|\mathbf{A}| \neq 0$, the equations $\mathbf{y} = \mathbf{A}\mathbf{x}$ can be solved in terms of determinants by what is known as *Cramer's rule*, namely $x_i = |\mathbf{A}_i| / |\mathbf{A}|$, where $\mathbf{A}_i$ is the matrix formed by replacing the ith column of **A** by the column vector **y**.

Cramer's rule gives an immediate expression for the elements of the inverse of **A** in terms of determinants. In fact, if $\mathbf{C} = \mathbf{A}^{-1}$,

$$c_{ji} = (-1)^{i+j} \frac{|\mathbf{A}_{ij}|}{|\mathbf{A}|},$$

where $\mathbf{A}_{ij}$ is the $(m-1) \times (m-1)$ matrix formed from **A** by deleting the ith column and the jth row. Notice the interchange of the suffices in c_{ji}.

Finally, if **A** is singular, there is at least one linear relationship expressing the values of a row of **A** in terms of the other rows. If there are k such relationships, expressing k of the rows in terms of the other $m - k$ (with $k \leqslant m - k$) **A** is said to be of *rank* $m - k$. In particular, if **A** is an estimated dispersion matrix (or correlation matrix, or S.O.P. matrix) based on q d.f., the rank is normally m or q, whichever is less.

E. PIVOTAL CONDENSATION

The usual elementary way of solving linear equations is by elimination. This is not the method generally used in computer programs for technical reasons; rounding off errors are apt to accumulate, and affect some of the coefficients calculated more than others, according to the order of elimination. Usually, therefore, successive approximation methods are preferred.

It is useful, however, to know the standard elimination method that was generally used to solve linear equations, and to invert matrices on electric calculating machines. Apart from its practical utility, it has the advantage, when used in multiple regression or in related multivariate techniques, of showing the effect of eliminating each variable in successive stages. It is also valuable in eliminating the effect of concomitant observations.

This method is known as pivotal condensation. Starting with the equation $\mathbf{y} = \mathbf{A}\mathbf{x}$, the first step is to eliminate x_1 and derive a new equation $\mathbf{y}_1 = \mathbf{A}_1\mathbf{x}_1$, relating the $m - 1$ remaining x's to the y's by a $(m - 1) \times (m - 1)$ matrix $\mathbf{A}_1$. In this equation:

$\mathbf{x}_1$ is the column vector with $m - 1$ elements $x_2 \ldots x_m$
$\mathbf{y}_1$ is the column vector with ith element $y_{i+1} - a_{i+1,1}y_1/a_{11}$
$\mathbf{A}_1$ is the $(m - 1) \times (m - 1)$ matrix with i,jth element

$$a_{i+1,j+1} - a_{i+1,1}a_{1,j+1}/a_{11}.$$

Thus the equation has been reduced by one order, and the process can be repeated until a single equation is reached, giving x_m in terms of the y's. The remaining x's are then found by substitution, x_{m-1} from the penultimate equation, and so on.

During the numerical calculations, it is wise to retain all the figures obtained. This guards against accumulating rounding off errors, and makes it easy to check the answer by a final substitution.

When the procedure is used for matrix inversion, the vector $\mathbf{y}$ is replaced by the unit matrix. Each column of the matrix is then treated in the same way as the column vector $\mathbf{y}$.

The element a_{11} in the first condensation is called the "pivot". It is convenient always to use the top left hand element as pivot, but of course the equations can always be rearranged to bring any element into this position. It is usually best to eliminate first variables that are obviously important; then if the remaining ones prove insignificant, they can be omitted without further calculations.

The following numerical example illustrates the method. It represents the calculations needed for finding a regression on three variables. The left hand matrix is a matrix of sums of squares and products; it is therefore symmetric; the elements below the principal diagonal are omitted for simplicity. The second condensation gives immediately the value of b_3; b_2 is then found by substituting in the first of the second set of equations, and b_1 by substituting in the first equation.

The last entry in the right hand column is the sum of squares of the dependent variable, and the changes in it in the successive stages show how much of the variability is accounted for by x_1, by x_2 after x_1 has been eliminated, and by x_3 after x_1 and x_2 have been eliminated.

$$\begin{pmatrix} 10 & 4 & -4 \\ & 15 & 8 \\ & & 20 \end{pmatrix} \begin{pmatrix} b_1 \\ b_2 \\ b_3 \end{pmatrix} = \begin{pmatrix} 5 \\ -10 \\ -10 \end{pmatrix}$$

$$\overline{50}$$

$$\begin{pmatrix} 13\cdot 4 & 9\cdot 6 \\ & 18\cdot 4 \end{pmatrix} \begin{pmatrix} b_2 \\ b_3 \end{pmatrix} = \begin{pmatrix} -12 \\ -8 \end{pmatrix}$$

$$\overline{47\cdot 5}$$

$$11\cdot 55 \ b_3 = \quad 0\cdot 59$$

$$\overline{37\cdot 13}$$

$$37\cdot 10$$

$$b_3 = \quad 0\cdot 051$$
$$b_2 = -0\cdot 930$$
$$b_1 = \quad 0\cdot 894$$

Check $\quad -4b_1 + 8b_2 + 20b_3 = -9\cdot 996$

Finally, the calculated values of b_1, b_2, and b_3 are checked by inserting them in the last of the original equations. If the result is correct, apart from the inevitable small rounding off error, the answer is accepted.

F. TRANSFORMATIONS AND CHANGE OF AXES

Suppose $\mathbf{x}$ represents the coordinates of a point related to ordinary mutually orthogonal coordinates in m-dimensional space. The equation $\mathbf{y} = \mathbf{Ax}$ can now be regarded as a change of axes, $\mathbf{y}$ representing the coordinates of the same point related to a new set of axes with the same origin. Now the distance of the point $\mathbf{x}$ from the origin is $\mathbf{x'x}$, and the distance in terms of the new coordinates is $\mathbf{y'y} = \mathbf{x'A'Ax}$. These two distances are equal for all points if $\mathbf{A'A} = \mathbf{I}$. This implies that the new axes are also mutually orthogonal, and that there has been no change of scale. It also implies that angles between directions are the same when related to the two sets of axes. A matrix $\mathbf{A}$ that satisfies $\mathbf{A'A} = \mathbf{I}$ is called *orthogonal*, and an equation relating two vectors via an orthogonal matrix is called an *orthogonal transformation*. (The term "unitary matrix" is also sometimes used. It has exactly the same meaning when applied to matrices with real elements, but is also defined for matrices with complex elements.)

Transformations of this sort, orthogonal and otherwise, play a large part in the mathematical treatment of multivariate data, and in interpretation and reification. The effect of transformations on quadratic forms is a principal consideration in many multivariate methods.

G. QUADRATIC FORMS

1. General

Any quadratic form can be written in the form $\mathbf{x}'\mathbf{A}\mathbf{x}$, where $\mathbf{x}$ is a column vector of m elements, and $\mathbf{A}$ is a $m \times m$ symmetric matrix. The coefficient of x_i^2 is a_{ii}, and that of $x_i x_j$ is $2a_{ij}$.

A quadratic form that is positive for all values of $\mathbf{x}$ except $\mathbf{x} = 0$ is called *positive definite*. One that is never negative, but can take a zero value for some non-zero values of $\mathbf{x}$, is called *positive semidefinite*. For example,

$$x_1^2 + 2x_1 x_2 + 2x_2^2$$

is positive definite, and

$$x_1^2 + 2x_1 x_2 + x_2^2$$

is positive semidefinite. The matrix of a positive definite form is non-singular; it is called a positive definite matrix. A positive semidefinite matrix is singular.

If $\mathbf{A}$ is positive definite, the equation $\mathbf{x}'\mathbf{A}\mathbf{x} = k$ represents an "ellipsoid" in m-dimensional space; that is, a surface bounded in all directions and not a surface analogous to a hyperboloid. If $\mathbf{A}$ is positive semidefinite, the ellipsoid is degenerate.

Any matrix of sums of squares and products, of variances and covariances, or of correlations, whether population values or estimates, is positive definite, or at least positive semidefinite.

This statement needs one qualification. It is true of estimated dispersion and correlation matrices when they are estimated in the usual way, from sums of squares and products; otherwise it may not be. One familiar example in which it may break down is when binary data are supposed to be based on threshold values of an underlying multivariate normal distribution. The correlation matrix may be estimated by finding the tetrachoric correlations from the various fourfold tables, but if this is done, it may not be positive definite or semidefinite.

For many purposes, it can be assumed that $\mathbf{A}$ is non-singular, and so positive definite. There are a few obvious exceptions; in a multivariate analysis of variance, the "between groups" matrix will certainly be singular if the degrees of freedom for groups are less than the number of variates.

2. Principal components

The principal component problem is that of finding an orthogonal transformation $\mathbf{y} = \mathbf{A}\mathbf{x}$ such that the y's are, in order, the combinations of

x's that give the largest, second largest, down to the smallest value to the quadratic form $\mathbf{a'Va}$, where $\mathbf{a}$ is a column of $\mathbf{A}$, and $\mathbf{V}$ is the dispersion matrix of the x's. The fact that the transformation is orthogonal implies that the new axes are at right-angles. Geometrically, the problem is that of identifying the values of k for which the ellipsoid $\mathbf{x'V^{-1}x} = k$ touches the sphere $\mathbf{x'x} = 1$; in other words, finding the directions of the axes of the ellipsoid.

Now the partial derivatives of $\mathbf{a'Va}$ with respect to the a's are the (doubled) elements of $\mathbf{Va}$, and the values of $\mathbf{a}$ that give extreme values of $\mathbf{a'Va}$ subject to $\mathbf{a'a} = 1$ satisfy $\mathbf{Va} - l\mathbf{Ia} = 0$, (or $\mathbf{a'V} - l\mathbf{a'I} = 0$), where l is an undetermined multiplier. This equation is obviously satisfied by $\mathbf{a} = 0$. If it is to have any solution other than this trivial one, the matrix $\mathbf{V} - l\mathbf{I}$ must be singular, and the determinant $|\,\mathbf{V} - l\mathbf{I}\,|$ must be zero.

This determinant is a pth order polynomial in l, and the equation thus has p roots. The fact that $\mathbf{V}$ is symmetric implies that they are all real, and the fact that it is positive definite implies that they are all positive. They are called the *latent roots* (or characteristic roots, or eigenvalues) of the matrix $\mathbf{V}$.

The case of equal roots presents some practical problems. It implies that the ellipsoid has a circular cross-section, so that the corresponding axes are indeterminate. For simplicity, assume that the roots are all distinct.

Now, to any value of l that satisfies $|\,\mathbf{V} - l\mathbf{I}\,| = 0$, there corresponds a value of $\mathbf{a}$ (unique except for sign) for which $(\mathbf{V} - l\mathbf{I})\mathbf{a} = 0$ and $\mathbf{a'a} = 1$, and for this value $\mathbf{a'Va} = l$. These values are called the standardized *latent vectors* (or characteristic vectors, or eigenvectors) of the matrix $\mathbf{V}$. They correspond to the directions of the axes of the ellipsoid, the largest value of l giving the longest axis, the second largest value the second longest, and so on. For a given value of l it is easy to find the corresponding latent vector by solving the simultaneous equations $(\mathbf{V} - l\mathbf{I})\mathbf{a} = 0$, imposing an arbitrary condition (say $a_1 = 1$) and then standardizing by multiplying by a constant factor.

Since $\mathbf{a}_i'\mathbf{Va}_j = l_i\mathbf{a}_i'\mathbf{a}_j = \mathbf{a}_i\mathbf{a}_j'l_j$, the assumption that the latent roots are distinct implies that $\mathbf{a}_i'\mathbf{a}_j = 0$, $i \neq j$, and so $\mathbf{A}$ is indeed an orthogonal matrix and $\mathbf{A'A} = \mathbf{I}$. Further, $\mathbf{AVA'} = \mathbf{L}$, where $\mathbf{L}$ is the $p \times p$ diagonal matrix with the values of l in the principal diagonal. Finally, it follows immediately from the equation $|\,\mathbf{V} - l\mathbf{I}\,| = 0$ that the sum of the values of l is the sum of the terms of the principal diagonal of $\mathbf{V}$ (known as the *trace* of $\mathbf{V}$, and written tr $(\mathbf{V})$). That is, the sum of the l's is the sum of the variances of the x's.

The problem of finding the numerical values of the latent roots can be solved in various ways. One of the most suitable for computer use depends on the fact that the latent roots of $\mathbf{V}^n$ are the nth powers of the latent roots of $\mathbf{V}$ since $(\mathbf{AVA'})^n = \mathbf{AV^nA'} = \mathbf{L}^n$. Thus if $\mathbf{V}$ is raised to a high power by repeated squaring, one of the latent roots, l_1^n, will be far larger than the others, and can be easily found. The process can then be repeated on $\mathbf{V} - l_1\mathbf{I}$ to find l_2, and so on.

In the case of equal roots, this procedure does not work so easily, but computer programs have special provisions to deal with such complications. There is no theoretical problem; the latent vectors and principal components corresponding to equal roots are indeterminate, but it is always possible to find an orthogonal set, and any such set will do.

Finally, consider the transformation $\mathbf{y} = \mathbf{Ax}$. Since $\mathbf{yy'} = \mathbf{Axx'A'}$, and the expected values of $\mathbf{yy'}$ and $\mathbf{xx'}$ are the respective dispersion matrices, the dispersion matrix of the y's is $\mathbf{L} = \mathbf{AVA'}$. Thus the y's are uncorrelated, and have variances equal to the values of the latent roots of $\mathbf{V}$. These are the principal components discussed in Chapter 3.

3. Canonical correlations

The problem of canonical analysis can be regarded as that of the simultaneous reduction of two symmetric matrices to diagonal form. Suppose, in the notation of Chapter 5, that $\mathbf{T}$ and $\mathbf{W}$ are symmetric positive definite matrices, and that $\mathbf{T} - \mathbf{W}$ is positive semidefinite. In the notation of Chapter 4, $\mathbf{T}$ and $\mathbf{W}$ are replaced respectively by $\mathbf{V}_{11}$ and $\mathbf{V}_{11} - \mathbf{V}_{12}\mathbf{V}_{22}^{-1}\mathbf{V}_{21}$. Now it is possible to find a matrix $\mathbf{A}$ such that $\mathbf{A'TA} = \mathbf{I}$, $\mathbf{A'(T-W)A} = \mathbf{L}$, where $\mathbf{L}$ is a diagonal matrix. The number of non-zero elements in the matrix $\mathbf{L}$ is the rank of $\mathbf{T} - \mathbf{W}$. This is either the number of variates p, or the degrees of freedom for groups q, whichever is less.

This result is known as Weierstrass's theorem (see Mirsky, 1955). When $\mathbf{T} - \mathbf{W}$ is non-singular, the values of l are the p roots of the determinantal equation $|\mathbf{B} - l\mathbf{T}| = 0$, where $\mathbf{B} = \mathbf{T} - \mathbf{W}$, or equivalently the latent roots of $\mathbf{BT}^{-1}$. When $\mathbf{B}$ is singular, some of these latent roots are zero. The canonical correlations are the square roots of the values of l, which are all positive. The equation $(\mathbf{B} - l\mathbf{T})\mathbf{a'} = 0$ defines a set of vectors $\mathbf{a'}$, and when $\mathbf{B}$ is non-singular, they define the matrix $\mathbf{A}$ as in the last section, and the canonical variables are defined as $\mathbf{y} = \mathbf{A'x}$. When $\mathbf{B}$ is singular, only the vectors corresponding to non-zero values of l are important; the remainder (which are, of course, indeterminate if there is more than one zero root) serve merely to complete the matrix $\mathbf{A}$.

In the general canonical correlation problem of Chapter 4, the stipulation that $p \leqslant q$ ensures that the $p \times p$ matrices are non-singular, unless some of the variables are perfectly correlated, or have zero variance in the sample. Then the matrix $\mathbf{A}$ is defined, and $\mathbf{A'x}$ and $\mathbf{A'y}$ give the canonical variables. The variables $\mathbf{a'x}$ are uncorrelated, the variables $\mathbf{a'y}$ are uncorrelated, and the only correlations between the two sets are between corresponding pairs. These correlations are the square roots of the corresponding l values.

Wilks' criterion L is equal to $\Pi(1 - l_i)$ and this is easily seen to be $|\mathbf{W}| / |\mathbf{T}|$, or $|\mathbf{V}_{11} - \mathbf{V}_{12}\mathbf{V}_{22}^{-1}\mathbf{V}_{21}| / |\mathbf{V}_{11}|$.

Appendix B

Multiple Regression

A. BASIC MATHEMATICS

Multiple regression, as a univariate technique, strictly falls outside the scope of this book. Nevertheless, so many of the classical methods of multivariate analysis are generalizations of multiple regression, or of univariate methods that are special cases of multiple regression, that it is perhaps helpful to summarize the main results.

Suppose y is a random variable distributed about a mean that is dependent on the values of p variables $x_1 \ldots x_p$. It is assumed that these variables affect only the mean of y, and in particular that the variance is constant. It is further assumed, in significance testing, that y is normally distributed about this mean. Finally, it is assumed that the mean can be regarded as a linear function of the x's—though, of course, there may be functional relationships among the x's, so that polynomial regression and other non-linear functions are covered by the general approach.

The problem is to find the best function of the form

$$Y = b_1 x_1 + \ldots + b_p x_p$$

to predict the mean value of y from the x's. This is done by least squares estimation, minimizing the residual sum of squares $\Sigma(Y-y)^2$. As is well known, this leads to a set of linear equations in the b's, the normal equations, of the form:

$$\mathbf{Sb = c}$$

where $\mathbf{S}$ is the matrix of sums of squares and products of the x's $\{S_{ij} = \Sigma(x_i - \bar{x}_i)(x_j - \bar{x}_j)\}$ and $\mathbf{c}$ is the vector of sums of products of the x's and y's $\{c_i = \Sigma(x_i - \bar{x}_i)(y - \bar{y})\}$. The constant term a is then simply $y - \mathbf{b'\bar{X}}$.

These estimates lead to an analysis of variance, dividing the total sum of squares of the y's, $T = \Sigma(y - \bar{y})^2$, into a sum of squares due to regression, $R = \mathbf{b'c}$, and an error sum of squares $E = T - R$. If there are N observations, and $n = N - 1$, the analysis takes the form:

	d.f.	S.O.S.	M.S.
Regression	p	R	
Error	$n - p$	E	s^2
Total	n	T	

This gives a test of significance for the relationship between y and $x_1 \ldots x_p$.

101

As is well known, the matrix $S^{-1}s^2$ gives the variances and covariances of the estimates $b_1 \ldots b_p$.

Suppose now that the p x's are divided into two groups, $x_1 \ldots x_k$ and $x_{k+1} \ldots x_p$. If regression on $x_1 \ldots x_k$ only gives a sum of squares Q, the difference $R-Q$ gives the sum of squares due to regression on $x_{k+1} \ldots x_p$ after taking account of the variables $x_1 \ldots x_k$. The analysis of variance thus gives a test of significance for the additional variables $x_{k+1} \ldots x_p$. The case $k = p-1$ naturally gives the same test of significance as that based on the standard error of b_p.

The analysis of variance takes the form:

	d.f.	S.O.S.	M.S.
Regression	k	Q	
$x_1 \ldots x_k$			
Additional	$p-k$	$R-Q$	
$x_{k+1} \ldots x_p$			
Error	$n-p$	E	s^2
Total	n	T	

This analysis can also be done the other way round, to give a significance test for $x_1 \ldots x_k$ after taking account of $x_{k+1} \ldots x_p$. These tests may lead to the conclusion that there is no point in including either one or the other set of variables.

Apart from the obvious application when the x's are observed variables, which may either be controlled by the experimenter of random variables recorded on the same items as y, there are other applications in which the x's are dummy variables representing a division into groups, or some other characteristic that is not obviously quantifiable. In the next section some of these applications will be briefly discussed.

B. MISCELLANEOUS APPLICATIONS

1. Analysis of experiments

In an ordinary randomized block experiment, there are b blocks, with $b-1$ corresponding degrees of freedom, and t treatments, with $t-1$ corresponding degrees of freedom. The analysis of the experiment may be regarded as a multiple regression, in which the block grouping is represented by $b-1$ dummy variables, and the treatments by a further $t-1$ dummy variables. For example, the block variables may take the value 1 in one block and zero elsewhere, for blocks $1 \ldots b - 1$. The treatment variables may be similarly coded, or, if the treatments are levels of a single factor, they may represent linear, quadratic, cubic . . . effects.

This type of regression analysis gives exactly the same analysis of variance as the usual method, which, of course, is simpler to carry out. The regression analysis, however, is much more general; it does not assume that each treatment occurs the same number of times in each block so that treatment and block effects are orthogonal. It is thus quite generally applicable to complicated designs in which, perhaps because of a large number of missing observations, blocks and treatments are not at all orthogonal. Thus the analysis of non-orthogonal designs presents no theoretical difficulty, although the computations may be heavy, and the coding of the dummy variables may make the data tape rather cumbersome.

2. Concomitant observations

In the analysis of Section A, the variables $x_1 \ldots x_k$ may represent concomitant observations, not themselves of direct interest, but important because they may affect the observations $x_{k+1} \ldots x_p$. In this case, the tests for the additional variables can be used to test whether there is any point in taking the concomitant observations into account, and whether, when they are taken into account, the main variables are related to the value of y.

An important special case is when the main variables are treatments, varieties, or some other form of grouping. In this case the analysis is equivalent to an analysis of covariance. The test for whether the concomitant observations have any effect when treatments have been taken into account is based on the "error" S.O.P. matrix, and the test for treatments corrected for concomitant observations is the usual final test for treatments in an analysis of variance and covariance.

One useful point to notice is that if the concomitant observations in an analysis of covariance themselves represent a grouping, the analysis can be done either way round. When there are many concomitant observations, the analysis of covariance involves handling rather large matrices, and the computations become heavy. Suppose there are three different treatments in an experiment on a group of animals drawn from ten different litters, and the experiment has not been designed so that treatments and litters are orthogonal. It is much easier to carry out an analysis of covariance within and between litters, regarding the treatments as concomitant, than the other way round. The two analyses are exactly equivalent. In the former case, the treatment sum of squares corrected for litter effects comes out as the regression term in the error sum of squares, and involves handling a 2×2 matrix, whereas in the latter, the correction for litters involves a 9×9 matrix. This technique of "dummy reversal" can often save a great deal of computation.

3. Dummy variables—special uses

Apart from their obvious applications to represent a grouping, such as blocks, treatments, sex, and so on, with a little ingenuity dummy variables can be used to simplify many statistical problems. For a fuller discussion, see Pearce (1965). Some examples of their use in the analysis of covariance in biological applications are:

(i) Missing values may be dealt with by using dummy variables taking the value 1 for the missing item and zero elsewhere.

(ii) A fertility trend that is not removed by the blocks may be at least partly corrected using a dummy variable increasing linearly in the direction of the trend.

(iii) The effect of disease or pests on a crop may be represented by an arbitrary score—but care is needed if the treatments could affect the concomitant observation.

C. SELECTION OF VARIABLES

A problem that is not completely solved is that of deciding which variables should be included in the final form of a regression equation and which should be rejected. A possible answer would be to say that a regression on k out of the total of p variables was ideal if:

(i) All regression coefficients were significant.

(ii) Any other choice of k variables gave a larger residual sum of squares.

(iii) The inclusion of any group of variables from the remaining $p - k$ did not give a significant reduction in the residual sum of squares.

There are, however, various difficulties in applying these criteria.

In the first place, the significance of a regression coefficient is a test on that variable alone; if p is large, it is probable that some variables will be judged significant (at, say, the 5% level) even if there is no relationship between the x's and y. An overall test of significance does not overcome the difficulty. When it has been shown that a relationship exists, the problem of rejecting irrelevant variables remains.

This is, of course, the same as the problem of multiple comparisons in the analysis of variance (see, for example, the discussion in Scheffé, 1959) and various procedures have been suggested for solving it. On the whole, however, it is usually better to retain irrelevant variables rather than reject important ones. In most applications, the level of significance is no more than a convenient yardstick for selection of variables, and if a regression coefficient is more than double its standard error, it is probably worthwhile at least retaining the corresponding variable for further consideration.

A second point is that the choice of variables may be affected by the nature of the variables themselves. If two variables are highly correlated and one is much easier to measure than the other, it will probably be preferred even if the other gives a slightly better prediction. Again, if three of the variables represent the linear, quadratic, and cubic components of a single factor, and only the third is judged significant, it may well be felt that this is probably a chance effect, and that none of them need be included. Many considerations of this sort may affect the choice of variables for regression, and they clearly cannot be incorporated in a single objective criterion.

Thirdly, the criterion suggested involves very extensive computations if p is large. To apply it strictly may require the calculation of $2^p - 1$ regression equations, and if p is of the order of 50, say, the problem becomes completely unmanageable.

Various suggestions have been made for finding reasonable approximations to the best solution. Studies of the clustering of variables (see Chapter 8) are one of the more promising approaches, but at present fully satisfactory methods have not been developed and tested.

The considerations of this section apply with equal force to the problem of the selection of variables in multivariate situations. Here, strict considerations of significance levels are still less important, but the standard error, when it is available, remains a useful guide.

Appendix C

Special Problems in Various Fields

A. INTRODUCTION

Multivariate analysis is based on certain standard methods, but it is seldom that a practical problem is exactly suited to a particular method. Often, information is available that cannot be incorporated in the numerical analysis. Sometimes there are relationships between the variables that cannot easily be expressed in numerical terms. Sometimes the variables are not all on the same footing, and some are known to be more important than others. Every problem has its own difficulties, and an automatic application of standard techniques is very likely to give misleading results.

It is impossible to discuss in detail all the problems that may arise in the interpretation of multivariate data. Blackith and Reyment (1971) gave nearly 800 references to papers using multivariate methods, and the total number published increases every month. Many of these papers suggest new methods, or refinements of established methods, for overcoming special difficulties. When faced with a problem in a particular field, it is wise to study, critically, as many as possible of the papers published on related problems.

Certain difficulties recur, however, in particular fields with such regularity that it is worth discussing them. Far too often, still, the methods used to analyse results are dependent not on the precise problem so much as on the computer programs available.

B. TAXONOMY

Numerical methods in taxonomy have fairly recently become popular. The problem of traditional taxonomy is, of course, one of classification. The taxonomist tries to find natural groups, suggesting relationships, among the items he is studying. This is the usual approach of the numerical taxonomist, but it has been suggested, for example by Du Praw (1965) that ordination is perhaps a more logical procedure. At least for certain groups, the attempt to force the results into the traditional hierarchical structure seems artificial.

The data used for taxonomy are largely binary. The basic assumption is that types differing in a large number of characteristics are further apart in the course of evolution than those that differ in a few respects. Much of the early work in numerical taxonomy was done on bacteria, and here the assumption seems, at least at first sight, reasonable. There is little information available about their evolution apart from what can be deduced from existing types, and geographical distribution, apart from the effects of the environment, has probably not much significance. With more highly developed organisms, however, the assumption is much less secure. It is well known that some characteristics are more reliable than others in indicating relationships, and it is difficult to incorporate this knowledge into the numerical analysis. Further, knowledge of the geographical distribution of the types being considered, and of the fossil record, can profoundly affect taxonomic conclusions. In these cases, to rely merely on numerical morphometrics is to ignore a great deal of the information available.

Another difficulty with taxonomic data is concerned with the idea of a sample. The hierarchical structure of traditional taxonomy seems to demand something like a significance test to demonstrate that genera, for example, are in some sense natural subdivisions of species, rather than a mere convenient dissection of the items. Normally, however, the data consist of all available types, perhaps of all known species in a group. It is straining the imagination too far to regard them as a random sample from a population, yet no satisfactory alternative has yet been suggested.

Finally, the "sample size" is often small. There are 2^p possible combinations of p binary variables, and there is normally at most one individual in each possible position, and none in most of them. Very commonly, some of the items are not precisely located, because of missing variables. It is usually unreasonable to assume that the variables are independent. In these circumstances, it is extremely difficult to justify the assertion that the clustering of the points is anything but a chance effect.

The validity of a taxonomic classification by numerical methods is commonly judged by comparing it with the current views of conventional taxonomists. It is hard to see that the great effort put into numerical taxonomy in the past few years has yet yielded much of value. For a full discussion, with many examples, see Blackith and Reyment (1971).

C. MEDICINE AND PSYCHIATRY

The multivariate problems arising in medicine and psychiatry have many features in common. Most of the signs and symptoms are binary. The data are not usually quite so sparse as in taxonomy, and there is a tendency for them to be clustered about the vertex representing no symptoms—cases showing a high proportion of the possible symptoms are comparatively rare.

In both, many concomitant observations are usually available. In medical applications, these represent personal characteristics, age, sex, and so on, which may affect the incidence of the symptoms. In psychiatry, the concomitant observations may include purely medical features; recent illness, chronic pains, and other strictly organic disorders may well affect the incidence of psychiatric symptoms. This point has been repeatedly emphasized, and it is perhaps worth mentioning a practical example. In an enquiry into a psychiatric disorder, the investigators concluded, on the basis of a cluster analysis, that there were two distinct groups. Four characters contributed most to the difference between the groups: age, sex, constipation and depression. This certainly suggests that elderly women tended to be constipated, and that elderly constipated women tended to be depressed, but does it really imply that there are distinct classes of the disorder?

Psychiatry is for the most part concerned with problems of classification of this sort. In medicine, discriminant analysis is also valuable, when exact diagnosis is possible, but not merely on the basis of signs and symptoms. The possibilities of computer diagnosis have attracted some attention recently.

D. PSYCHOLOGY

Many multivariate problems of all types arise in the various branches of psychology. Animal behaviour, involving the sort of situation in which various stimuli can give rise to various responses, provides examples of canonical analysis. Problems about the effect of environment or education on the opinions or activities of different groups can be analysed by discriminant analysis. Problems of ordination and classification arise in many different situations.

Factor analysis was, of course, developed in connexion with a particular psychological problem, and has since been very widely used. Perhaps it is still too widely used; it is important to relate any factor analysis to the precise structure postulated by the analysis, and in many cases the assumptions implied are obviously inappropriate.

An interesting feature of modern psychological statistics has been the development of non-parametric techniques. So far, not many specifically multivariate methods of this sort have been proposed, but psychological data are commonly of a non-parametric type—either ranks or scores on a more or less arbitrary scale. These can be usually handled by classical methods without much risk of misleading results. Care is needed, as always, in problems of classification.

E. SOIL SCIENCE

The preparation of maps to show, not the value of a single variable, but some composite features related to geographical position, involves multivariate problems. A typical example of this situation is the preparation of general purpose soil maps. The same sort of problems are involved in mapping ecological, anthropological, or economic data.

The first step is usually the division of the data into classes. As a rule, this is a matter of dissection rather than classification in the sense of finding a natural subdivision. The overriding consideration is the utility of the resulting map, rather than the identification of modes in the distribution, and in any case it is rare that the data can be regarded as a random sample from a natural population.

One question that has not been much considered is how far geographical position should affect the allocation of items. Clearly if sufficient information were available it might be desirable to do some sort of smoothing of the data to avoid too many isolated points, unconnected with any other point in the same category. One possibility would be to incorporate geographical distance in a distance measure used for dissection purposes (Webster and Burrough, 1973). Another suggestion (Marriott, 1971) is to replace the original observations by those functions of them which best correlate with a set of variables representing the geographical coordinates, and then perform the dissection on the new variables.

Another feature of observations on soil is that they are commonly taken at several different depths. Typically, one might take the same set of, say, a dozen observations at each of three different depths. Each location would then be represented by 36 readings, falling naturally into groups of three, observations of the same character at three different depths. This special relationship between the observations cannot easily be taken into account, and in practice they are usually treated simply as 36 separate variates.

Sometimes soils are strongly stratified, and this raises further problems. If observations are taken at several different depths, there is a choice of procedures.

(i) The readings may be taken at fixed depths. If these readings are used as the data for dissection, there will appear to be a sharp change in soil type whenever the boundary between two strata crosses one of the chosen depths, although there is no sharp corresponding change in the character of the soil.

(ii) The soil may be divided into "horizons", and the reading associated with, say, the first three horizons. Here there seems to be a sharp change between two soils that are identical except for a very thin top layer covering one of them. The depth of the horizons cannot easily be incorporated into the analysis.

When soils are not strongly stratified, treating observations at different depths as if they were quite separate seems to be satisfactory. For the stratified case, the problem is much less easy. Perhaps the answer may lie in some more or less subjective measure of distance or similarity.

F. ARCHAEOLOGY

Rather surprisingly, numerical methods have been widely used in investigating archaeological problems. The questions that usually arise are those of classification, dissection, or ordination of items of different sorts. These may be more or less simple artifacts, quantified in terms of their various features, or they may be sites or graves with data of the artifacts found in them.

Geographical position may be important. Either depth, or, as in the case of the cemetery at Münsingen (Sibson, 1972), the site of the find, may give a very good indication of age. This may be supplemented by various chemical and physical methods of dating.

The main difficulty in applying numerical methods in archaeology, as in taxonomy, is that of incorporating all the available information, in a logical way, in a mathematical analysis. Standard techniques are not designed to accommodate data of so varied a type, and it is necessary to discard information that does not admit of ready quantification, or that is not on the same footing as the other data. It is certainly interesting that often numerical analysis based on such incomplete information is in good agreement with the conclusions of archaeologists reached independently, but this sort of result is more encouraging to the numerical analyst than valuable to the archaeologist.

References
and Author Index

The page on which a reference occurs is given in square brackets; P indicates Preface.

ANDERSON, J. A. (1974). (In preparation.) [49, 78]
ANDREWS, D. F. (1972). Plots of high-dimensional data. *Biometrics* **28**, 125–136. [9]
ANDREWS, D. F., GNANADESIKAN, R. and WARNER, J. L. (1971). Transformations of multivariate data. *Biometrics* **27**, 825–840. [17]
ASHTON, E. H., HEALY, M. J. R., OXNARD, C. E. and SPENCE, T. F. (1965). The combination of locomotor features of the primate shoulder girdle by canonical analysis. *J. Zool.* **147**, 406–429. [83]
BARNARD, M. M. (1935). The secular variations of skull characters in four series of Egyptian skulls. *Ann. Eugen.* **6**, 352–371. [79, 81]
BARTLETT, M. S. (1935). Contingency table interactions. *Suppl. Jl R. statist. Soc.* **2** 248–252. [78]
BARTLETT, M. S. (1938). Further aspects of the theory of multiple regression. *Proc. Camb. phil. Soc. math. phys. Sci.* **34**, 33–44. [29, 46]
BARTLETT, M. S. (1947a). The use of transformations. *Biometrics* **3**, 39–52. [17]
BARTLETT, M. S. (1947b). Multivariate analysis. *Suppl. Jl R. statist. Soc.* **9**, 176–197 [30, 81]
BARTLETT, M. S. (1951). The effect of standardization on a χ^2 approximation in factor analysis. *Biometrika* **38**, 337–344. [21]
BARTLETT, M. S. (1954). A note on the multiplying factors for various χ^2 approximations. *Jl R. statist. Soc.* (B) **16**, 296–298. [21]
BLACKITH, R. E. (1962). L'identité des manifestations phasaires chez les acridiens migrateurs. *Colloques int. Cent. natn. Rech. scient.* **114**, 299–310. [52]
BLACKITH, R. E. and REYMENT, R. A. (1971). "Multivariate Morphometrics." Academic Press, London and New York. [50, 52, 54, 58, 66, 106, 107, P]
COX, D. R. (1972). The analysis of multivariate binary data. *Appl. Statist.* **21**, 113–120. [78]
DAY, N. E. (1969). Estimating the components of a mixture of normal distributions. *Biometrika* **56**, 463–474. [69]
DU PRAW, E. J. (1965). Non-Linnean taxonomy and the systematics of honey-bees. *Syst. Zool.* **14**, 1–24. [75, 106]
EDWARDS, A. W. F. and CAVALLI-SFORZA, L. L. (1965). A method for cluster analysis. *Biometrics* **21**, 362–375. [63]
FISHER, R. A. and YATES, F. (1938). "Statistical Tables for Biological, Agricultural and Medical Research." Oliver and Boyd, Edinburgh. [5, 17]
FRIEDMAN, H. P. and RUBIN, J. (1967). On some invariant criteria for grouping data. *J. Am. statist. Ass.* **62**, 1152–1178. [53, 72]

GOWER, J. C. (1966). Some distance properties of latent root and vector methods used in multivariate analysis. *Biometrika* **53**, 325–338. [24]

GOWER, J. C. (1967). Multivariate analysis and multidimensional geometry. *Statistician* **17**, 13–28. [50]

GOWER, J. C. (1969). The basis of numerical classification. *Syst. Assoc. Publ.* **8**. [52]

HARTIGAN, J. A. (1973). Minimum mutation fits to a given tree. *Biometrics* **29**, 53–65. [66]

HILLS, M. (1966). Allocation rules and their error rates. *Jl R. statist. Soc.* (B) **28**, 1–31. [40]

HOPE, K. (1968). "Methods of Multivariate Analysis." University of London, Athlone Press, London. [P]

HOTELLING, H. (1931). The generalisation of "Student's" ratio. *Ann. math. Statist.* **2**, 360–378. [30]

JARDINE, N. and SIBSON, R. (1970). "Mathematical Taxonomy." Wiley, London and New York. [54, 58]

KENDALL, D. G. (1971). Construction of maps from "odd bits of information". *Nature, Lond.* **231**, 158–159. [56, 57]

KENDALL, D. G. (1972). Contribution to discussion on a paper by Sibson, R. (1972). *Jl R. statist. Soc.* (B) **34**, 338–349. [56]

KENDALL, D. G. (1974). "Data-analytic problems in archaeology and history." Proc. European Meeting of Statisticians, Budapest (to appear). [56]

KENDALL, M. G. and STUART, A. (1968). "The Advanced Theory of Statistics", Vol. 3 (2nd edition). Griffin, London. [5, 20, 38, 47, 59, 62, P]

KRUSKAL, J. B. (1964). Multidimensional scaling by optimizing goodness-of-fit to a nonmetric hypothesis. *Psychometrika* **29**, 1–27. [56]

LAWLEY, D. N. (1940). The estimation of factor loadings by the method of maximum likelihood. *Proc. R. Soc. Edinb.* **60**, 64–82. [36]

LAWLEY, D. N. (1956). Tests of significance for the latent roots of covariance and correlation matrices. *Biometrika* **43**, 128–136. [21]

LAWLEY, D. N. and MAXWELL, A. E. (1963, 1970). "Factor Analysis as a Statistical Method." (1st and 2nd editions.) Butterworths, London. [47, 48, 49]

LAZARSFELD, P. F. and HENRY, N. W. (1968). "Latent Structure Analysis." Mifflin, Boston, U.S.A. [49, 76]

MARRIOTT, F. H. C. (1952). Tests of significance in canonical analysis. *Biometrika* **39**, 58–64. [30, 80]

MARRIOTT, F. H. C. (1971). Practical problems in a method of cluster analysis. *Biometrics* **27**, 501–514. [53, 73, 74, 86, 109]

MIRSKY, L. (1955). "An Introduction to Linear Algebra." Clarendon Press, Oxford. [100]

PEARCE, S. C. (1965). "Biological Statistics." McGraw-Hill, New York. [103, P]

PEARSON, E. S. and HARTLEY, H. O. (eds.) (1972). "Biometrika Tables for Statisticians", Vol. 2. Cambridge University Press, Cambridge. [17, 29, 30, 80]

PENROSE, L. S. (1954). Distance, size and shape. *Ann. Eugen.* **18**, 337–343. [22]

RAO, C. R. (1950). Statistical inference applied to classificatory problems. *Sankhyā* **10**, 229–256. [36]

RAO, C. R. (1965). "Linear Statistical Inference and its Applications." Wiley, New York. [36, 48, P]

RAO, C. R. amd MITRA, S. K. (1971). "Generalized Inverse of Matrices and its Applications." Wiley, New York. [94]

REYMENT, R. A. (1969). Some case studies of the statistical analysis of sexual dimorphism. *Bull. geol. Instn Univ. Uppsala* **1**, 75–81. [52]

RICHARDS, L. E. (1972). Refinement and extension of distribution-free discriminant analysis. *Appl. Statist.* **21,** 174–176. [38]

RUBIN, J. (1967). Optimal classification into groups; an approach for solving the taxonomy problem. *J. theor. Biol.* **15,** 103–144. [63, 74]

SCHATZOFF, M. (1966). Exact distributions of Wilks's likelihood ratio criterion. *Biometrika* **53,** 347–358. [29]

SCHEFFÉ, H. (1959). "The Analysis of Variance." Wiley, New York. [16, 104]

SCOTT, A. J. and SYMONS, M. J. (1971). Clustering methods based on likelihood ratio criteria. *Biometrics* **27,** 387–397. [73]

SIBSON, R. (1972). Order invariant methods for data analysis. *Jl R. statist. Soc.* (B) **34,** 311–349. [16, 54, 109]

SOKAL, R. R. (1961). Distance as a measure of taxonomic similarity. *Syst. Zool.* **10,** 70–79. [52]

SOKAL, R. R. and SNEATH, P. H. A. (1963). "Principles of Numerical Taxonomy." Freeman, San Francisco [86]

SPEARMAN, C. (1904). General intelligence objectively determined and measured. *Am. J. Psychol.* **15,** 201–293. [44]

THURSTONE, L. L. (1947). "Multiple Factor Analysis." Chicago University Press, Chicago. [49]

WEBSTER, R. (1972). Wilks's criterion: a measure for comparing the value of general purpose soil classifications. *J. Soil. Sci.* **22,** 254–260. [85]

WEBSTER, R. and BURROUGH, P. A. (1973). Computer-based soil mapping of small areas from sample data. *J. Soil Sci.* **23,** 210–234. [75, 85, 87, 109]

WILKS, S. S. (1935). On the independence of *k* sets of normally distributed statistical variables. *Econometrica* **3,** 309–326. [29]

WINSTEN, C. B. and SAVIGEAR, F. (1966). The use of rooms and the use of land for housing. *Jl R. statist. Soc.* (A) **129,** 157–208. [6, 8]

WISHART, J. (1928). The generalized product-moment distribution in samples from a multivariate normal population. *Biometrika* **20A,** 32–52. [15]

WISHART, D. (1968). "A Fortran II Program for Numerical Classification." St. Andrews University, St. Andrews. [71]

Index

An entry in *italics* indicates the beginning of a section on the topic.